How to Speak Shakespeare

by Cal Pritner and Louis Colaianni

SANTA
MONICA
PRESS

Published by:
SANTA MONICA PRESS LLC
P.O. Box 1076
Santa Monica, CA 90406-1076
1-800-784-9553
www.santamonicapress.com
books@santamonicapress.com

Printed in the United States

Santa Monica Press books are available at special quantity discounts when purchased in bulk by corporations, organizations, or groups. Please call our Special Sales department at 1-800-784-9553.

This book is intended to provide general information. The publisher, author, distributor, and copyright owner are not engaged in rendering health, medical, legal, financial, or other professional advice or services. The publisher, author, distributor, and copyright owner are not liable or responsible to any person or group with respect to any loss, illness, or injury caused or alleged to be caused by the information found in this book.

ISBN 1-891661-18-3

Library of Congress Cataloging-in-Publication Data

Pritner, Cal, 1935-
     How to speak Shakespeare / Cal Pritner and Louis Colaianni
       p. cm.
     Includes bibliographical references
     ISBN 1-891661-18-3
     1. William Shakespeare, 1564-1616—Language. 2. English language—Early modern, 1500-1700—Spoken English. 3. English language—Early modern, 1500-1700—Pronunciation. 4. Oral interpretation of poetry. 5. Acting. I. Colaianni, Louis, 1959- II. Title.

     PR3072 .P75 2001
     427'.009'03—dc21

                     2001040027

Book and cover design by cooldogdesign
Cover photo of Cal Pritner by Larry Levenson Photography
Cover photo of Louis Colaianni by Judson Morgan

Contents

This book is dedicated to
Evamarii Johnson and David Golston

Acknowledgements

We thank the students of the UMKC Department of Theatre graduate acting program and the California State Summer School for the Arts for their participation in the development of this book. We are also grateful to our many colleagues for advice and encouragement along the way; particularly, Theodore Swetz, Dale AJ Rose, Jennifer Martin, Joseph Price and Felicia Londre.

Foreword

This book is the culmination of over twenty years of teaching and research into the challenge of how to speak Shakespeare. We have dedicated ourselves to a basic challenge: how to help actors communicate Shakespeare's ideas and stories clearly for audiences. *How to Speak Shakespeare* features a step-by-step process for speaking Shakespeare clearly and intelligently, using only one Shakespeare play for its examples: *Romeo and Juliet*.

Our process is based on sound yet simple principles that have proven effective for a wide range of students: from eighth graders to undergraduate theatre majors to MFA students to professional actors. It's been "classroom-tested" and "rehearsal-tested" in schools and theatres from coast to coast including: Illinois State University, the Illinois Shakespeare Festival, the Missouri Repertory Theatre, the California Institute of the Arts, the University of Missouri-Kansas City, the California State Summer School for the

Arts, and the American Conservatory Theatre. It has also been taught to faculty leaders of the International Thespian Society from across America.

In our effort to make *How to Speak Shakespeare* as accessible as possible, we make no assumptions about what you "know" about Shakespeare. We offer "Additional Background" in case you've forgotten the difference between Elizabethan and Jacobean, or between a "First Folio" and a "Quarto." Except for a copy of *Romeo and Juliet*, no "accessories" are required.

So, let's get to work! It's Shakespeare and it's worth the effort.

Cal Pritner
Louis Colaianni

Introduction

The Basic Sequence

Step One: Test Your Understanding.

Shakespeare's words are four hundred years old, and they often don't have the same meaning today as they did back then. How do you deal with this?

a) Look it up in the dictionary.

Eventually you'll want to check some words out in the *Oxford English Dictionary* (your local college, high school, or public library should have the OED in print or on cd-rom), but for our demonstration exercises, you won't have to.

b) Paraphrase.

Try saying it in your own words, as closely to the text's meaning as you can get; that's the way to make sure you're understanding what you're saying.

Step Two: Stress for Meaning.
a) Find the rhythms.

Most of Shakespeare is written in verse. We'll help you find the verse's rhythm.

b) Syncopate for meaning.

We'll show you how to vary the rhythm of the verse, or "syncopate" it, for meaning and communication.

Step Three: Celebrate the Poetry.

Shakespeare wrote poetically. In order to give full expression to Shakespeare's poetry, the actor/character must be aware of basic expressive tools that the text employs.

a) Use the Punctuation.

Understanding Shakespeare's punctuation helps the actor speak the text meaningfully. Carefully followed, Shakespeare's punctuation provides a roadmap for the organization of characters' thoughts. In many cases it also dictates rhythmic shifts in the text.

b) Repeated Sounds.

The characters play with repeated sounds. Repeated sounds, including "rhyme," "assonance," and "alliteration" are clues for meaning and expression.

c) Connecting the Key Words and Phrases.

Key words include:

1) Action words (usually verbs).

2) Naming words (usually nouns)

3) Amplifying, explaining, and contrasting words, such as "auncient" and "new" or "civill hands" and civill bloud"

What Shakespeare Do We Use?

The plays were written in the late 1500s and early 1600s, printed in a typeface that's hard to read today. Most of the Shakespeare you've read has been "edited" and "improved" for modern readers, not for actors.

In fact, over the past four hundred years, editors have re-spelled the text, re-punctuated the text, even changed the words, especially in the really popular plays like *Romeo and Juliet*.

In this workbook, we use the original text, but in modern type. That's the only change we make from the original text. We retain Shakespeare's original punctuation and spelling. We believe actors should use the original text because it's punctuated for breathing, speaking, and acting aloud.

The first exercise—the "Chorus" speech—is the first speech from the earliest printed version of Romeo and Juliet: the "quarto" version.

What is a "quarto"? What is a "folio"?

The terms "quarto" and "folio" refer to the size of a book. "Quarto"-size books are approximately five by seven inches. They are printed on sheets of large paper folded twice (into quarters—thus "quarto"); eighteen of Shakespeare's plays were published during his life in quarto versions. Folio refers to plays printed on large sheets of paper which are folded only once. "Folio" books are roughly twice as large as "quartos." In 1623, the collected plays of William Shakespeare were published in a "folio" edition. There were subsequent editions of the folio, therefore, the first edition is referred to as the "first folio."

There are several facsimile editions of Shakespeare's first folio available; for more information, see our Selected Bibliography at the end of the book.

Chorus

In the quarto of *Romeo and Juliet*, the Chorus is the first actor to appear on stage. The Chorus's speech is a good starting point for our process. In ancient Greek plays, in addition to the actors playing characters there is often a group of actors called a "chorus." The chorus directly addresses the audience, commenting on the play's events. In several plays, Shakespeare used the device of a chorus (usually played by one actor) to deliver a prologue.

Because the Chorus begins the play, no previous knowledge of the story is necessary. In this play, the Chorus can be thought of as an actor, not yet in character, who comes before the audience to focus their attention on the story they are about to see. The actor playing the Chorus enters the stage, looks directly at the audience and speaks a clever and well-memorized poem which s/he knows the audience will find a useful introduction to the play.

This speech is reprinted from one of the earliest editions of *Romeo and Juliet* and some of the spellings look strange to the modern reader. For example, the words "civil" and "ancient" contain extra letters: "civill" and "auncient." The word "households" is spelled without an "e": "housholds." In time your eye will adjust to these archaic spellings but, context will also aid you in recognizing these words. For more information on archaic spellings, see pages 21–22.

1. Two housholds both alike in dignitie,

2. (In faire Verona where we lay our Scene)

3. From auncient grudge, breake to new mutinie,

4. Where civill bloud makes civill hands uncleane:

5. From forth the fatall loynes of these two foes,

6. A paire of starre-crost lovers, take their life:

7. Whose misadventur'd pittious overthrowes,

8. Doth with their death burie their Parents strife.

9. The fearful passage of their death-markt love,

10. And the continuance of their Parents rage:

11. Which but their childrens end nought could remove:

12. Is now the two houres trafficque of our Stage.

13. The which if you with patient eares attend,

14. What heare shall misse, our toyle shall strive to mend.

Step One: Test Your Understanding

Word Meanings

Some editions of *Romeo and Juliet* will provide meanings for obscure words. We advise not trusting them. Frankly, we've found some are misleading.

When possible, look up as many words as you can in the *Oxford English Dictionary (OED)*. Here's what happened when we looked up "households" from line one of the Chorus:

Meaning One: "The 'holding' or maintaining of a house or family; housekeeping: domestic economy." Almost, but not quite.

Meaning Two: "The contents or appurtenances of a house collectively." No, not quite.

Meaning Three: "The inmates of a house collectively; an organized family, including servants or attendants, dwelling in a house; a domestic establishment."

This is it!

Why worry over the differences? Because words are important in Shakespeare, and we must know what the words mean, very specifically.

The key: we've chosen from several specific meanings. We've chosen among options. We haven't fooled ourselves into assuming we "know" what the word meant in Shakespeare's time.

Yes, we acknowledge that an actor who's playing a huge role can't look up every noun and every verb. But, while you're working here, try doing it as much as you can. Learn to use the *OED*. It will pay off in specificity.

Example: "Dignitie"

Line Two: "dignitie."

Meaning One: "quality of being worthy or honourable; worthiness, worth, nobleness, excellence."

Meaning Two: "honourable or high estate, position, or estimation; honour; degree of estimation, rank."

Frankly the differences aren't great. The idea is that both houses are thought "worthy," or "honourable." But now we're confident of the meaning in context.

Example: "Where"

The Chorus says the two households break to new mutiny "*where* civill bloud makes civill hands uncleane:"

The *OED* gives us many definitions of "where," and in several of them it's clear that "where" in older times was used often in the sense of "in or at which." We sometimes still use "where" that way today (to mean "which"), but today, dictionaries consider it non-standard or incorrect usage.

However, for our purposes we can paraphrase "where" as "in which." Paraphrase it as: "two households break to new mutiny *in which* civill bloud makes civill hands uncleane."

Archaic Words and Forms of Words

The modern form of the word "drive" in the simple past tense is "drove." But in Shakespeare's time it could also be "drave": "A troubled mind drave me to walk abroad."

Some words and expressions are no longer used, such as this greeting: "Godgigoden." This word is not as nonsensical as it looks. It is actually a contraction of "God give thee good evening," or, "**God gi**(ve)(thee)**go**(o)**d**(ev)en(ing)."

The capital "I" can be used to spell both the personal pronoun, "I," and an affirmative response, today spelled as "Aye."

Here are some modern forms paired with archaic forms of words as found in *Romeo and Juliet*:

more/mo
struck/strooken
film/phliome
ribbon/riband
burden/burthen
murder/murther
he/a
cloth/clout
month/moneth
umpire/umpeere

What Have We Learned?

Whenever possible take the time to look the word up in the *OED*. That way you can be sure you're using it the way Shakespeare intended (and as the character you will be using language with specificity).

Exercise: Paraphrase

Paraphrase the following lines in your own words as specifically as possible. Come as close as you can, in your words, to Shakespeare's meaning. Then compare your paraphrase with our paraphrases that follow.

1. Two housholds both alike in dignitie,

2. (In faire Verona where we lay our Scene)

3. From auncient grudge, breake to new mutinie,

4. Where civill bloud makes civill hands uncleane:

5. From forth the fatall loynes of these two foes,

6. A paire of starre-crost lovers, take their life:

7. Whose misadventur'd pittious overthrowes,

8. Doth with their death burie their Parents strife.

9. The fearful passage of their death-markt love,

10. And the continuance of their Parents rage:

11. Which but their childrens end nought could remove:

12. Is now the two houres trafficque of our Stage.

13. The which if you with patient eares attend,

14. What heare shall misse, our toyle shall strive to mend.

Our Paraphrase

1. *Two housholds both alike in dignitie,*
2. *(In faire Verona where we lay our Scene)*
3. *From auncient grudge, breake to new mutinie,*
4. *Where civill bloud makes civill hands uncleane:*

Paraphrase:

1. Two extended families, equal in estimation,
2. (In beautiful Verona, the city where our play is set)
3. Out of very old ill-will, emerge in a fresh battle,
4. In which citizens' bleeding results in dirtied citizens:

5. *From forth the fatall loynes of these two foes,*
6. *A paire of starre-crost lovers, take their life:*
7. *Whose misadventur'd pittious overthrowes,*
8. *Doth with their death burie their Parents strife.*

Paraphrase:

5. Out of the deathly heritage of the two enemies,
6. Two ill-fated, infatuated persons, kill themselves:
7. The lovers' unfortunate, sad to behold, outcomes,
8. Upon their dying, submerge the warfare between their families.

9. *The fearfull passage of their death-markt love,*
10. *And the continuance of their Parents rage:*
11. *Which but their childrens end nought could remove:*

12. Is now the two houres trafficque of our Stage.

Paraphrase:
9. The terrible ending of their ill-fated romance,
10. And the incessant fight between their families:
11. Nothing but the lovers' deaths could end:
12. Is what this play's 120 minute passage in the theatre
is about.

13. The which if you with patient eares attend,
14. What heare shall misse, our toyle shall strive to mend.

Paraphrase:
13. This is the subject, that if you listen with attention,
14. But lose catching something, our work will try to
correct.

Paraphrasing is not an exact science. Often, the exact
word choice is at the discretion of the paraphraser. To illustrate
this point, the authors of this workbook each paraphrased
the Chorus speech. Compare the paraphrase above with the
paraphrase below. It is our hope that sharing two paraphrases
with you will help you realize that your choices, provided
they clearly tell the story, without omitting details, are just
as valid as ours.

1. Two extended families of equal status,

2. (In beautiful Verona, the place where our play is set)

3. Out of an old feud, start a new fight,

4. In which the blood of some residents makes the hands of other residents dirty:

5. Each of the two revengeful families gives birth,

6. Their unlucky children fall in love with each other and kill themselves:

7. The children's unfortunate, sad, struggles,

8. When they die, end the fighting between their families.

9. The terrible shocking story of their fatal love,

10. And the unceasing fighting between their families:

11. Which nothing except the death of these children could end:

12. Is the two hour long action of this play.

13. If you listen patiently to the rest of our play,

14. Any part of the story you have missed in my prologue, our acting will try to make up for.

Oral Exercise:
Meaning and Communication

1. Compare your paraphrase and ours. Which do you prefer? Be honest with yourself, and be specific. Do you understand it all? If not, keep digging at the meanings.

2. Read the "Chorus" aloud now. If possible, read it to another person, concentrating on meaning and communication.

Advice: this is a poem, not dialogue. Read it aloud as if it's a poem you've written, and you're really proud of the writing and how it prepares the audience to see the play.

1. Two housholds both alike in dignitie,

2. (In faire Verona where we lay our Scene)

3. From auncient grudge, breake to new mutinie,

4. Where civill bloud makes civill hands uncleane:

5. From forth the fatall loynes of these two foes,

6. A paire of starre-crost lovers, take their life:

7. Whose misadventur'd pittious overthrowes,

8. Doth with their death burie their Parents strife.

9. The fearful passage of their death-markt love,

10. And the continuance of their Parents rage:

11. Which but their childrens end nought could remove:

12. Is now the two houres trafficque of our Stage.

13. The which if you with patient eares attend,

14. What heare shall misse, our toyle shall strive to mend.

Step Two: Stress for Meaning

Iambic Pentameter: The Basic Rhythm

English is a language which we speak with greater and lesser emphasis on syllables; we <u>EM</u> pha <u>SIZE</u> some <u>SYLL</u> a <u>BLES</u> and not others.

Most of Shakespeare's verse dialogue (characters speaking in poetry) is written in lines of ten syllables with the potential to emphasize every-other-syllable:

ta <u>DA</u>, ta <u>DA</u>, ta <u>DA</u>, ta <u>DA</u>, ta <u>DA</u>.

In this rhythmic pattern, an unstressed syllable (ta), is followed by an stressed syllable (<u>DA</u>). Each "ta <u>DA</u>" is called a "foot." The use of the term "foot" began in ancient Greece when poetic rhythms were derived from dance rhythms. There are five "feet" in every line. Here are the first two lines of the Chorus. Note the five numbered feet of each line:

1   2   3   4   5

Two <u>HOUS</u> / holds <u>BOTH</u> / a <u>LIKE</u> / in <u>DIG</u> / ni <u>TIE</u>

(In <u>FAIRE</u> / Ve <u>RON</u> /a <u>WHERE</u> / we <u>LAY</u> / our <u>SCENE</u>)

In each line, there are ten syllables, and every-other-syllable is stressed. We call this a "regular" line; it's regular in that the pattern of stresses continues consistently (without variation). It is "ta <u>DA</u>" "ta <u>DA</u>" throughout the line.

This combination of an unstressed syllable followed by a stressed syllable is called an "iamb." And it's called "pentameter" because it is the "ta <u>DA</u>" pattern, repeated five times (as in "Pentagon," a five-sided building). The name may not be important, but the concept of the "ta <u>DA</u>," repeated, is important. It's the basic structure of Shakespeare's verse. It's a kind of "time signature" for the verse, like music having a 4/4 time signature. We won't encourage you to speak Shakespeare in a mind-numbing, sing-song, ta <u>DA</u>, ta <u>DA</u>, ta <u>DA</u>, ta <u>DA</u>, ta <u>DA</u>. But it is important for you to recognize the time signature, the basic structure, so you can determine when and why rhythmic variations must occur for clarity of meaning.

Below is the Chorus speech with all the stressed syllables of the iambic pentameter in underlined, capital letters.

1. Two HOUSholds BOTH aLIKE in DIGniTIE,

2. (In FAIRE VeROna WHERE we LAY our SCENE)

3. From AUNcient GRUDGE, breake TO new MUtiNIE,

4. Where CIvill BLOUD makes CIvill HANDS unCLEANE:

5. From FORTH the FAtall LOYNES of THESE two FOES,

6. A PAIRE of STARRE-crost LOvers, TAKE their LIFE:

7. Whose MISadVENtur'd PIttious OVerTHROWES,

8. Doth WITH their DEATH buRIE their PArents STRIFE.

9. The FEARful PAssage OF their DEATH-markt LOVE,

10. And THE conTINuANCE of THEIR paRENTS rage:

11. Which BUT their CHILDrens END nought COULD reMOVE:

12. Is NOW the TWO houres TRAfficque OF our STAGE.

13. The <u>WHICH</u> if <u>YOU</u> with <u>PA</u>tient <u>EARES</u> at<u>TEND</u>,

14. What <u>HEARE</u> shall <u>MISSE</u>, our <u>TOYLE</u> shall <u>STRIVE</u> to <u>MEND</u>.

Note that if "regularly" pronounced, "bu<u>RIE</u>," in line number eight, sounds quite strange. Likewise, "con-<u>TIN</u>u<u>ANCE</u>," in line number ten, disturbs the line's rhythms. Both words are irregularities that we'll address later, on pages 34 and 37.

A Crash Course in Syllable Stress

In two-syllable words, only one syllable is stressed. "Housholds" is a two-syllable word. The first syllable has the stress: <u>HOUS</u>holds.

"Alike" is a two-syllable word in which the second syllable has the stress: a<u>LIKE</u>.

You probably notice that we have been underlining and capitalizing the stressed syllable. We have done this for the purposes of our mark-up system. Dictionaries, however, use an accent mark (`) to indicate the stressed syllable:

`house holds

a `like

In words of three or more syllables there can be primary and secondary stresses.

"Dignitie" is a three-syllable word in which the first syllable has the primary stress. The third syllable has the secondary stress. The middle syllable is unstressed.

`dig nit `ie

"Verona" is a three-syllable word in which the middle syllable is stressed; there is no secondary stress in this word. The two surrounding syllables are unstressed.

Ve `ron a

Although dictionaries use accent marks (as above), at this point we will use an <u>underline</u> and CAPITALIZATION for the stressed syllable(s).

Contracted Words

If we pronounce "continuance" in line ten in a normally stressed manner, "conTINuANCE," it doesn't fit the iambic pentameter rhythm. If we contract it to a three-syllable word, "conTINyins," it fits the iambic perfectly. Contractions of this sort, creating surprising pronunciations, happen occasionally in Shakespeare. We believe the reader/actor should be aware of them. Please speak the words and phrases below and make sure you can hear the difference.

Usual pronunciation:
conTINuANCE

Pronunciation which fits verse in *Romeo and Juliet* Chorus:
conTINyins

Here is line ten from the Chorus. Notice how skewed the meter is when "continuance" is treated as a four syllable word:
And THE conTINuANCE of THEIR paRENTS rage

Here is the same line, but it treats "continuance" as a three-syllable word. Notice how this renders the line "regular":
And THE conTINyins OF their PArents RAGE

Here are a few other examples of words which are contracted in the Chorus. Now that you know what to look for, you'll find many other examples throughout the plays:

Word in Chorus	Non-contracted Pronunciation	Contracted Pronunciation
piteous	PIteeuhs	PIchus
toil	TOIyuhl	TOIL
hours	OWwerz	OWRZ

A Central Concept:
Syncopate for Meaning

One of the principal ideas of this book is that the regular "ta <u>DA</u>, ta <u>DA</u>," unbroken, is "mind and ear numbing." Regularity of the iambic pentameter can put the ear and the mind to sleep. We believe the actor/character must offset it, or "syncopate for meaning."

We believe you can best syncopate for meaning by putting primary stress on verbs and nouns, especially verbs. Why? Because verbs and nouns are the language's primary carriers of oral meaning.

To syncopate, in music, is to accent beats that aren't normally/regularly accented. In other words, to syncopate is to take a "beat" that's regular, and to break it up with irregular accents.

Central to communicating meaning, defeating the potentially "mind numbing" iambic (ta <u>DA</u>, ta <u>DA</u>), is the creation of stresses tied to meaning, or "syncopations for meaning." How do we syncopate for meaning? By stressing the verbs and nouns with extra emphasis.

By "stressing verbs and nouns," we don't necessarily mean to say them louder than the other words in a phrase. After all, a pattern of alternately loud and soft volume will become just as mind-numbing. Think of all the different ways there are to make a word stand out. It can be said higher or lower in pitch than the words surrounding it. It can be said with softer volume, or a whisper. It can be said with a bend in pitch. Just remember to use the type of emphasis which will best convey meaning. Volume is merely one of many ways to emphasize, to "syncopate for meaning."

Why stress verbs and nouns? Because verbs are the action sources of our language. As action words, verbs power the language. They identify what's being done. Nouns also power the language by identifying persons, things, and places. They power the verbs, or the verbs act upon them. So, we syncopate by emphasizing action verbs and nouns, usually with slightly greater emphasis on the verbs.

Oral Exercise: Regular vs. Syncopated

We have pointed out that line eight of the Chorus could be interpreted as "regular," in that it could be said:

Doth <u>WITH</u> their <u>DEATH</u> bur<u>IE</u> their <u>PA</u>rents <u>STRIFE</u>.

However, not only does this "regular" pattern require an odd pronunciation of "burie," it draws the ear away from the key words. How do we solve this? By reading the line aloud with syncopated stress, emphasizing verbs and nouns. **Note that, as discussed above, only one syllable is stressed in two-syllable verbs and nouns:**

Doth with their <u>DEATH</u> <u>BUR</u>ie their <u>PA</u>rents <u>STRIFE</u>. (Syncopated)

We hope very much that you "hear and feel" the difference between the "(Regular)" and the "(Syncopated)" reading. If not, try it again, because it's central to our whole system.

Once again, read the line in straight, or regular, iambic pentameter and compare it with our "(Syncopated)" version:

Doth <u>WITH</u> their <u>DEATH</u> bur<u>IE</u> their <u>PA</u>rents <u>STRIFE</u>. (Regular)

Doth with their <u>DEATH</u> <u>BUR</u>ie their <u>PA</u>rents <u>STRIFE</u>. (Syncopated)

Which reading makes more sense to you? Why? Be certain you hear the differences between the "regular" and the "syncopated" lines. The process we are introducing depends on your hearing this difference.

We think speaking it in the syncopated way makes more sense than it does with the "regular" iambic stress. The meaning of the sentence is carried by "death burying parents strife," and we pronounce the verb <u>BUR</u>ie, rather than the "regular" bu<u>RIE</u>. We've syncopated for meaning.

Verbs: They Power Ideas

A central premise of this workbook and of our process is that active verbs are the power-source of language, and that when Shakespeare is spoken aloud, verbs must be given highest importance. A notable exception to this is the verb "to be" (see below); as a rule, "to be" should not receive the stress we give to action verbs.

For those who don't remember their grammar, here are some examples of verbs:

The verb "Lay": <u>Lay</u> the book on the table.

The verb "Break": The class will <u>break</u> for recess.

The verb "Make": This process will <u>make</u> the text clearer.

The verb "Take": <u>Take</u> the money.

Refresher Course in the Verb "To Be"

In our mark-up system, the most important stress is given to verbs. However, exceptions are made for forms of the verb "to be." The verb "to be" is a way of describing a "state of being." It is not an action or active verb. In our system of syncopating for meaning, only active verbs, verbs describing action, are syncopated, or given primary stress. So, it's important to identify which verbs are forms of the verb "to be" and should not be underlined, or stressed, when syncopating the text aloud. Common forms of the verb "to be" include: is, am, are, were, will be, going to be, etc. For those of you who may be shaky on your grammar, we've included a brief explanation of the verb "to be." For more detailed information, consult a grammar manual.

The form of the verb "to be" is based upon tense (past, present or future) and person-first person (I), second person (you), third person (s/he, they, it).

Present Forms

is, am, are:
I <u>am</u>, s/he <u>is</u>, it <u>is</u>, you <u>are</u>, they <u>are</u>, we <u>are</u>

Past Forms

was, were:
I <u>was</u>, s/he <u>was</u>, it <u>was</u>, they <u>were</u>

Future Forms

will be, going to be:
I <u>will be</u>, I am <u>going to be</u>

Some Other Unstressed Verbs

When verbs such as "do," "have," and such auxiliary verbs as "would," are used to modify the main verb (such as "go," in the examples below), they should not be emphasized.

Verbs with "do": I do <u>go</u>, I did <u>go</u>

Verbs with "have/has": I have <u>gone</u>, She has <u>gone</u>

Auxiliary Verbs (should, would, could, etc.): I should <u>go</u>, I could <u>go</u>, I would <u>go</u>, I may <u>go</u>/I might <u>go</u>.

A Mark-up System:
Underline to Syncopate, Part One

As part of a mark-up system for actors, we'll double underline each verb, in order to give verbs greater emphasis than nouns. The double underline is a way to help you visualize the importance of fully stressing the verbs.

1. Two housholds both alike in dignitie,

2. (In faire Verona where we lay our Scene)

3. From auncient grudge, breake to new mutinie,

4. Where civill bloud makes civill hands uncleane:

5. From forth the fatall loynes of these two foes,

6. A paire of starre-crost lovers, take their life:

7. Whose misadventur'd pittious overthrowes,

8. Doth with their death burie their Parents strife.

9. The fearful passage of their death-markt love,

10. And the continuance of their Parents rage:

11. Which but their childrens end nought could remove:

12. Is now the two houres trafficque of our Stage.

13. The which if you with patient eares a<u>ttend</u>,

14. What heare shall <u>misse</u>, our toyle shall <u>strive</u> to <u>mend</u>.

Oral Exercise: Emphasize the Verbs

Read the Chorus speech aloud, emphasizing the verbs. Don't bother with "acting." Merely make certain you're concentrating on the verbs as the primary source of meaning.

Nouns: They are the Namers

Your next step will be to underline every noun in the speech, once. Nouns are the second most important words for meaning; in general, they should be emphasized more than other words, but just slightly less than verbs.

Refresher Course in Nouns

Nouns name persons, places, and things. They can be "proper names"—that is the actual name of a person or a place, such as "Verona," or "Juliet"—or they can be the word by which we call a person or a thing, such as "city," "girl," etc. A "thing" can be a literal object such as a window, or it can be an idea or concept such as "dignitie." Below are a few examples of nouns. For more detailed information, consult a grammar manual.

Person: Juliet, maid, servant, Lord, Lady.

Place: Verona, orchard, house.

Thing (literal object): window, sword, poem, book.

Thing (concept or idea): dignitie, grudge, mutinie, overthrow.

A Mark-Up System:
Underline to Syncopate, Part Two

We need to stress the most important words in a phrase in order to clarify meaning; we do this by stressing ("syncopating") the verbs and nouns. To visualize the syncopation for verbs and nouns, we've <u>underlined</u> the nouns once and signified the primacy of the verbs by <u>double-underlining</u> them:

1. Two <u>housholds</u> both alike in <u>dignitie</u>,

2. (In faire <u>Verona</u> where we <u>lay</u> our <u>Scene</u>)

3. From auncient <u>grudge</u>, <u>breake</u> to new <u>mutinie</u>,

4. Where civill <u>bloud</u> <u>makes</u> civill <u>hands</u> uncleane:

5. From forth the fatall <u>loynes</u> of these two <u>foes</u>,

6. A <u>paire</u> of starre-crost <u>lovers</u>, <u>take</u> their <u>life</u>:

7. Whose misadventur'd pittious <u>overthrowes</u>,

8. Doth with their <u>death</u> <u>burie</u> their <u>Parents</u> <u>strife</u>.

9. The fearful <u>passage</u> of their death-markt <u>love</u>,

10. And the <u>continuance</u> of their <u>Parents</u> <u>rage</u>:

11. Which but their <u>childrens</u> <u>end</u> nought could <u>remove</u>:

12. Is now the two <u>houres</u> <u>trafficque</u> of our <u>Stage</u>.

13. The which if you with patient <u>eares</u> <u>attend</u>,

14. What heare shall <u>misse</u>, our <u>toyle</u> shall <u>strive</u> to <u>mend</u>.

We <u>hope</u> the <u>effect</u> of <u>giving</u> extra <u>stress</u> to <u>verbs</u> by <u>underlining</u> them twice <u>helps</u> you <u>see</u> their <u>importance</u> in <u>syncopating</u> for <u>meaning</u>.

The ta DA ta DA <u>pattern</u> of the <u>verse</u> is present. But <u>underlining</u> <u>verbs</u> and <u>nouns</u> <u>helps</u> you <u>syncopate</u> or <u>break-up</u> the <u>regularity</u> of the <u>iambic</u> <u>pentameter</u>.

Oral Exercise: Verbs and Nouns

Earlier you read aloud for meaning, concentrating on verbs. Now go through the Chorus speech on pages 45–46, reading aloud with greatest emphasis on the verbs, and the second-greatest emphasis on the nouns. Again, don't act it; as you read aloud, merely concentrate on communicating meaning.

The principle is: Learn to stress both verbs and nouns, almost always putting slightly more stress on the verb than on the noun. This is a guide to communication. This relative emphasis helps the audience "get" the ideas you're expressing. Occasionally there will be exceptions; but this system of emphasis is dependable in helping the audience understand meaning.

Remember, stress the verbs most, and stress the nouns almost as much!

Important note: Obviously, in underlining verbs and nouns with a double underline or a single underline, we are not urging you to put equal emphasis on all syllables. As noted above in "A Crash Course in Syllable Stress" (page 33), in the case of multi-syllable verbs and nouns such as "remove" and "dignity," you must emphasize the primary stressed syllable of the word: "re `move," "`dig ni ty." To stress all syllables equally in these words would sound rather strange. Therefore, remember that although we ask you to underline the entire verb or noun, the primary stressed syllable must receive the greatest emphasis.

Knowing When to Break the Rules

Now that you have put the rule of stressing "verbs" and "nouns" into practice, it is important to know that this rule is made to be broken. Sometimes another part of speech will need to be emphasized for meaning, perhaps a preposition, adverb or adjective. Remember that stressing the verbs most and the nouns second most is *usually* the clearest way to say the line. But context will *sometimes* tell you that to under-emphasize another kind of word in favor of verbs and nouns will obscure the meaning. Here are some examples of lines which require the primary stress on a different part of speech than the verb and the noun:

1) In this dialogue between two Capulet servants, Samson and Gregory, there is word play based on the similarity in sound among colliers (coal miners), choler (anger) and collar (as in shirt collar). In Gregory's second line, it is necessary to emphasize the preposition "out" more than the verbs and nouns, in order to maximize the word play:

Samson: <u>Gregory</u>, on my <u>word</u>, we'll not <u>carry</u> <u>coales</u>.

Gregory: No, for then we should be <u>colliers</u>.

Samson: I <u>mean</u>, an we be in choler, we'll <u>draw</u>.

Gregory: Ay, while you <u>live</u>, <u>draw</u> your <u>neck</u> OUT of the <u>collar</u>.

2) In the following dialogue between Benvolio and Romeo, in order to make the clear distinction between being

in love and being out of love, Romeo needs to stress the word "am" in his second line. This goes directly against our general rule not to emphasize forms of the verb to be. Remember, it is an uncommon exception, but we think in this case (as elsewhere) the exception maximizes meaning:

Benvolio: In <u>love</u>?

Romeo: Out.

Benvolio: Out of <u>love</u>?

Romeo: Out of <u>favour</u>, where I AM in <u>love</u>.

3) In the Nurse's remembrance of weaning Juliet as a toddler, she must emphasize the adjective "bitter" in order to maximize meaning. (Note that the nurse follows the custom of referring to small children as "it" rather than "he" or "she."):

Nurse: ...When it did <u>taste</u> the <u>wormwood</u> on the <u>nipple</u>

Of my <u>dug</u> and <u>felt</u> it BITTER, pretty <u>fool</u>,

To <u>see</u> it tetchy and <u>fall</u> out with the <u>dug</u>.

4) Sometimes, we find clarity is enhanced when two or more words are combined to create a single noun or verb. We'll call these "compound" verbs and nouns. Here are some examples of compound nouns from the chorus speech. Each one combines an adjective with a noun. They should be spoken as one long noun.

civill hands

civill bloud

star-crost lovers

death-markt love

Here are some examples of compound verbs from *Romeo and Juliet*. They are usually composed of a verb and a preposition, which together form one long verb.

cast it off

send it back

beats down

Step Three: Celebrate the Poetry

Shakespeare was a *poet* who was writing for the theatre, not for readers. As a poet he celebrated the sounds of words, and celebrated the interplay of sound and meaning. So, we must pay attention to the patterns of his sounds in the way we would with any poetry, especially patterns of repeated sounds.

The most prominent repeated sounds in Shakespeare are the rhyming line endings. Early in his career he wrote in rhyme frequently. But, in our process of finding ways to stress and emphasize Shakespeare for oral meaning, we find that stressing the rhyme often diminishes communication of ideas. Instead, we recommend syncopating by emphasizing verbs, nouns, and contrasts. In fact, we find that the rhyme scheme in Shakespeare sounds so strongly that even when unemphasized the audience hears it.

Use the Punctuation

The Shakespeare text we are using throughout this workbook is taken from the original printings of *Romeo and Juliet* in Shakespeare's day, the folio and quarto. This makes our text quite different from today's "edited versions," versions that are re-spelled, re-punctuated, and sometimes sanitized against vulgar meanings. Modern editors are known to have substituted alternative words, spellings and punctuation marks for those that Shakespeare may have "meant." These substitutions were made with the reader, not the actor, in mind.

We believe the actor should start work with the punctuation of Shakespeare's time (the folio and the quartos) and we recommend that the actor use the "original" punctuation as a guideline for communication.

We acknowledge that in Shakespeare's time punctuation, like spelling, was sometimes a "creative" act as well as a thing of some systematic usage. Nevertheless, after years of study in the classroom, in rehearsal halls, and in performance, we believe there are useful guidelines to apply to his punctuation. We believe the "original" punctuation was often intended for the actor's eye, literally as cues for the actor, and therefore we urge that you attend to punctuation in the process of creating sound and sense. Below are some guidelines for interpreting the punctuation on Shakespeare's plays:

In the early printed texts, (quartos and folios), punctuation seems to be used to map out thought progressions. Shakespeare's punctuation can be broken down into a hierarchy: from commas (which are the weakest indications of thought progression), to semi-colons (which are stronger than commas), to colons (which are even stronger), to periods (which indicate a complete stop).

• Commas (,) set ideas apart, but they don't necessarily indicate pauses. If you pause for every comma, you'll break up the stream of thought, and diminish communication.

Speak the following speech of Romeo, using the commas as visual signs of thought shifts, but taking no more than a tiny pause, if you take any pause at all:

Romeo: Arise fair Sun and kill the envious Moon,
　　　 Who is alreadie sicke and pale with griefe,
　　　 That thou her Maide art far more faire then she:

• Semicolons (;) seldom appear, and they are often used as they are today: To indicate the connection between two related ideas.

Speak Romeo's following lines using the semi-colon as a connection between two related ideas. How can you convey this through rhythm and inflection?

Romeo: Alacke there lies more peril in thine eye,
　　　 Then twenty of their swords; looke thou but sweete,
　　　 And I am proofe against their enmity.

• Colons (:) are used much differently from today. In Shakespeare's texts the colon seems to complete an idea and signal the charge into the next idea with new energy.

Speak Romeo's following speech, using the colon to indicate the completion of one idea as you charge on to the next idea. How can you convey this through rhythm and inflection?

Her eye discourses I will answer it:
I am too bold 'tis not to me she speakes:
Two of the fairest starres in all the heaven,
Having some business do entreat her eyes,
To twinckle in their Spheres till they return.

• Periods (.) are used to complete an idea, a complete sentence, in the same way they are today.

Speak Juliet's line and use the period as a completion of the sentence. Inflect the final word with downward finality:

... be but sworne my love,
And Ile no longer be a Capulet.

• Paragraphs: In long speeches, punctuation can be used to identify the organization of oral "paragraphs." The colon is used to signal several independent clauses; and then, when a major idea is completed, and thought shift occurs, it is signaled with a period. Below we have broken a continuous speech into "paragraphs."

Benvolio:

(Statement Main Idea):
Tybalt, here slain, whom Romeo's hand did slay.

(first paragraph):
Romeo, that spoke him fair, bid him bethink
How nice the quarrel was, and urg'd withal
Your high displeasure.

(second paragraph):

All this uttered

With gentle breath, calm look, knees humbly bow'd

Could not take truce with the unruly spleen

Of Tybalt, deaf to peace, but that he tilts

With piercing steel at bold Mercutio's breast,

Who, all as hot, turns deadly point to point

And, with a martial scorn, with one hand beats

Cold death aside, and with the other sends

It back to Tybalt, whose dexterity

Retorts it.

(third paragraph):

Romeo, he cries aloud

'Hold, friends! Friends part!' and swifter than his tongue

His agile arm beats down their fatal points

And 'twixt them rushes; underneath whose arm

An envious thrust from Tybalt hit the life

Of stout Mercutio; and then Tybalt fled.

(fourth paragraph):

But by and by comes back to Romeo,

Who had but newly entertaine'd revenge,

And to't they go like lightening: for, ere I

Could draw to part them, was stout Tybalt slain,

And as he fell did Romeo turn and fly.

(fifth paragraph):

This is the truth or let Benvolio die.

Oral Exercise: Punctuation

Follow the directions for punctuation as you read the Chorus speech aloud, concentrating on the syncopations (the emphasis on verbs and nouns). In addition, follow the directions in the margin for punctuation. Pay special attention to the colon (:). Remember, it is a signal to complete an idea but charge on to the next idea with new energy. Remember also not to pause for each comma; notice the comma, but only pause slightly if at all.

1. Two housholds both alike in dignitie,
comma, small shift in thought *(a)*

2.(In faire Verona where we lay our Scene)
parenthetical statement, change vocal register *(b)*

---

3. From auncient grudge, breake to new mutinie,
comma, small shift in thought *(a)*

---

4. Where civill bloud makes civill hands uncleane:
*colon, finish one thought and charge on with new energy
to the next one* *(b)*

---

5. From forth the fatall loynes of these two foes,
comma, small shift in thought *(c)*

---

6. A paire of starre-crost lovers, take their life:
*comma, small shift in thought, followed by colon, finish one
phrase and charge on with new energy into the next phrase* *(d)*

---

7. Whose misadventur'd pittious overthrowes,
comma, small shift in thought (c)

---

8. Doth with their death burie their Parents strife.
Period, FULL STOP, (largest shift in thought). (d)

---

9. The fearful passage of their death-markt love,
comma, small shift in thought (e)

---

10. And the continuance of their Parents rage:
colon, finish one phrase and charge on with new energy to the next phrase (f)

---

11. Which but their childrens end nought could remove:
colon, finish one phrase and charge on with new energy to the next phrase (e)

---

12. Is now the two houres trafficque of our Stage.(f)
Period, FULL STOP, (largest shift in thought)

---

13. The which if you with patient eares attend,
comma, small shift in thought (g)

14.What heare shall misse, our toyle shall strive to mend.
comma, small shift in thought, followed by period, FULL STOP, (largest shift in thought) (g)

Repeated Sounds

Poets "play" with words and the sounds of words in combination. The three most common ways in which poets play with sounds are:

- Alliteration, the repetition of consonants:

    <u>f</u>rom <u>f</u>orth the <u>f</u>atal loins of these two <u>f</u>oes

- Assonance, the repetition of vowel sounds:

    from <u>au</u>ncient grudge br<u>ea</u>k to n<u>ew</u> m<u>u</u>tinie

- Repeated words:

    Where <u>civill</u> bloud makes <u>civill</u> hands uncleane

- Internal rhyme, the repetition of the final sounds of a word *contained within a line*:

    In <u>faire</u> Verona, <u>where</u> we lay our Scene

- Rhymed line endings, the repetition of the final sounds of a word *at the end of the line*:

    The which if you with patient eares att<u>end</u>,
    What here shall misse, our toyle shall strive to m<u>end</u>.

Shakespeare wrote mostly in "blank verse." This is the term for verse which does not rhyme. However, some of

Shakespeare's verse, especially in his poems and early plays, does rhyme. In his Sonnets, Shakespeare uses a pattern in which alternating lines rhyme. The pattern in which lines of verse are rhymed is called a "rhyme scheme." For example, the rhyme scheme of the first four lines of the Chorus speech (below) is marked A B A B, to indicate that the first line (A), rhymes with the third line (also marked A), and that the second line (B) rhymes with the fourth line (also marked B).

Two housholds, both alike in dignitie   (A)

(In faire Verona, where we lay our Scene)   (B)

From ancient grudge, break to new mutinie   (A)

Where civill bloud makes civill hands uncleane: (B)

In the next four lines of the Chorus speech, Shakespeare continues the alternating rhyme scheme. Because brand new rhyming sounds are introduced, the rhyme scheme continues CDCD:

From forth the fatall loynes of these two foes,   (C)

A paire of starre-crost lovers, take their life: (D)

Whose misadventur'd pittious overthrowes,   (C)

Doth with their death burie their Parents strife.   (D)

In the following four lines the rhyme scheme continues in the same way, with new rhyming sounds, and the rhyme scheme is marked EFEF. Note: "love" forms an imperfect rhyme with "remove" in general American English.

The fearful passage of their death-markt <u>love</u>,   (E)

And the continuance of their Parents <u>rage</u>:   (F)

Which but their childrens end nought could <u>remove</u>:(E)

Is now the two houres trafficque of our <u>Stage</u>.   (F)

When two adjacent lines rhyme, it is called a "couplet." The rhyme scheme of the last two lines of the Chorus speech is a couplet. It is marked GG:

The which, if you with patient eares attend,   (G)

What heare shall misse, our toyle shall strive to mend.(G)

Syllables that rhyme stand out, catch the listener's ear, and can help syncopate the verse. But, it is our advice to let rhyme take care of itself. Rhyme is so orally powerful that in most cases it need not be emphasized. Usually you will find that in order to communicate you must make an effort to emphasize other elements, the verbs, nouns, balances, and non-rhyming repeated sounds. But you must know the rhyme is there.

Oral Exercise: Shakespeare's Verse

In the following chart, we have indicated the various types of repeated sounds which occur in the Chorus speech. After reading it over, practice the speech out loud, with an awareness of the rhymes and other repeated sounds.

Repeated Sounds

---

1. Two housholds both alike in dignitie,

(a)

---

2. (In faire Verona where we lay our Scene)
(internal rhyme: faire/where)   *(b)*

---

3. From auncient grudge, breake to new mutinie,

(a)

---

4. Where civill bloud makes civill hands uncleane:
(repeated word: civill)   *(b)*

---

5. From forth the fatall loynes of these two foes,
(repeated f)   *(c)*

---

6. A paire of starre-crost lovers, take their life:
internal rhyme (paire/their and repeated st)   *(d)*

---

7. Whose misadventur'd pittious overthrowes,
(repeated z: whose/overthrowes),
(repeated s: misadventur'd/pittious)   *(c)*

---

8. Doth with their death burie their Parents strife.
(repeated d and th)   *(d)*

---

9 The fearful passage of their death-markt love,
(love, line 9, & re<u>move</u>, line 11, may be called archaic or
partial rhyme).   *(e)*

---

10. And the continuance of their Parents rage:
                                                           (f)

---

11. Which but their childrens end nought could remove:
                                                           (e)

---

12. Is now the two houres trafficque of our Stage.
(repeated vowel sound: now/houres)   *(f)*

---

13. The which if you with patient eares attend,
(internal rhyme: eares/heare)   *(g)*

---

14. What heare shall misse, our toyle shall strive to mend.
(repeated m)   *(g)*

Connecting the Key Words and Phrases

Part of the task of syncopating for meaning is the act of identifying how words and phrases relate to each other. Sometimes a word or phrase will "amplify," or "explain" another word or phrase: The <u>boy</u> in the <u>green shirt</u>, — "green shirt" amplifies, or explains who the "boy" is. In this case the words "boy" and "green shirt" must be stressed in order for the listener to follow the thread of the thought. When these stresses cause us to deviate from the iambic pentameter in Shakespeare's verse, we have once again syncopated for meaning.

Amplifying, or, explaining words and phrases:
In the phrase "two housholds, both alike in dignitie," "housholds" is amplified, or, explained by "alike in dignity."
In the phrase "In faire Verona where we lay our scene," "scene," explains, or amplifies "Verona."

Contrasting words or phrases:
Sometimes we syncopate by "contrasting" words or phrases: Not <u>that car</u>, the <u>other one</u>, —the words "that car" contrast with "other one."
In the phrase "Where civill hands make civill bloud uncleane," "civill hands," contrasts with "civill bloud."

Oral Exercise: Make the Connection

In this chart, we have indicated the various amplifying, explaining, and contrasting words and phrases which occur in the Chorus speech. Speak the speech aloud using the italicized notes below each line to help you connect the key words and phrases. Follow the thread of the thought by stressing the amplifying, explaining, and contrasting words, even when this causes a deviation from the rhythms of iambic pentameter. Once again, you are syncopating for meaning. Because this exercise emphasizes amplifying, explaining, and contrasting, we are not asking you to focus on nouns and verbs. We'll ask you to put it all together later:

1. Two housholds both alike in dignitie,
*"housholds" is explained or amplified by "both alike
in dignitie"*   *(a)*

---

2. (In faire Verona where we lay our Scene)
"Scene" explains, or amplifies, "Verona"   *(b)*

---

3. From auncient grudge, breake to new mutinie,
*("ancient" contrasts with "new"; "grudge" contrasts with
"mutinie")*   *(a)*

---

4. Where civill bloud makes civill hands uncleane:
("civill blood" contrasts with "civill hands")   *(b)*

---

5. From forth the fatall loynes of these two foes,
*("from forth the fatal loins" (birth) contrasts with "take
their life" (death))*
("two foes" contrasts with "a paire of starre crost lovers") (c)

---

6. A paire of starre-crost lovers, take their life:
(d)

---

7. Whose misadventur'd pittious overthrowes,
(c)

---

8. Doth with their death burie their Parents strife.
("their death" contrasts with "parent's strife") (d)

---

9. The fearful passage of their death-markt love,
("death-markt" amplifies, or explains "love") (e)

---

10. And the continuance of their Parents rage:
("parent's rage" contrasts with "children's end") (f)

---

11. Which but their childrens end nought could remove:
(e)

---

12. Is now the two houres trafficque of our Stage
(f)

---

13. The which if you with patient eares attend,
("attend" contrasts with "misse") (g)

---

14. What heare shall misse, our toyle shall strive to mend. (*"patient ears attend" is amplified, or explained by "our toyle shall strive to mend."*) (*g*)

Let's Review

Up to now we've introduced one-by-one the elements of our system for marking the Shakespearean text for sound and sense. Now it's time for you to try and put it all together. Complete the following exercise and compare it to our mark-up on pages 70–71.

Exercise: Your Mark-Up

Underline Verbs Twice, Nouns Once
Make Note of Repeated Sounds
Amplifying, Explaining, and Contrasting Words and Phrases

1. Two housholds both alike in dignitie,

(a)

_____

2. (In faire Verona where we lay our Scene)

(b)

_____

3. From auncient grudge, breake to new mutinie,

(a)

_____

4. Where civill bloud makes civill hands uncleane:

(b)

_____

5. From forth the fatall loynes of these two foes,

(c)

_____

6. A paire of starre-crost lovers, take their life:

(d)

_____

7. Whose misadventur'd pittious overthrowes,

(c)

_____

8. Doth with their death burie their Parents strife.

(d)

9. The fearful passage of their death-markt love,

(e)

10. And the continuance of their Parents rage:

(f)

11. Which but their childrens end nought could remove:

(e)

12. Is now the two houres trafficque of our Stage.

(f)

13. The which if you with patient eares attend,

(g)

14. What heare shall misse, our toyle shall strive to mend.

(g)

Our Mark-Up

Underline Verbs Twice, Nouns Once
Make Note of Repeated Sounds
Amplifying, Explaining, and Contrasting Words and Phrases

1. Two <u>housholds</u> both alike in <u>dignitie</u>,
("housholds" is explained or amplified by "both alike in dignitie")   *(a)*

---

2. (In faire <u>Verona</u> where we <u>lay</u> our <u>Scene</u>)
(internal rhyme: faire/where)   *(b)*

---

3. From ancient <u>grudge</u>, <u>breake</u> to new <u>mutinie</u>,
("ancient" contrasts with "new"), ("grudge" contrasts with "mutinie")   *(a)*

---

4. Where civill <u>bloud</u> <u>makes</u> civill <u>hands</u> uncleane:
(repeated word: civill), ("civill blood" contrasts with "civill hands")   *(b)*

---

5. From forth the fatall <u>loynes</u> of these two <u>foes</u>,
(repeated f "from forth the fatal loins," or birth, and contrasts with "take their life," or death), ("two foes" contrasts with "a paire of starre crost lovers")   *(c)*

---

6. A <u>paire</u> of starre-crost <u>lovers</u>, <u>take</u> their <u>life</u>:
(internal rhyme: paire/their), (repeated st)   *(d)*

---

7. Whose misadventur'd pittious <u>overthrowes</u>,
*(repeated z: whose/overthrowes), (repeated s: misadventur'd/
pittious)*   *(c)*

---

8. Doth with their <u>death</u> <u>burie</u> their <u>Parents</u> <u>strife</u>.
*(Repeated d and th), ("their death" contrasts with "parent's
strife")*   *(d)*

---

9. The fearful <u>passage</u> of their death-markt <u>love</u>,
*(<u>love</u>, line 9, & <u>remove</u>, line 11, may be called archaic or par-
tial rhyme), ("death-markt" amplifies, or explains "love") (e)*

---

10. And the <u>continuance</u> of their <u>Parents</u> <u>rage</u>:
("parent's rage" contrasts with "children's end")   *(f)*

---

11. Which but their <u>childrens</u> <u>end</u> nought could <u>remove</u>:
     (e)

---

12. Is now the two <u>houres</u> <u>trafficque</u> of our <u>Stage</u>.
(repeated vowel sound: now/houres)   *(f)*

---

13. The which if you with patient <u>eares</u> <u>attend</u>,
*(internal rhyme: eares/heare), ("attend" contrasts with
"misse"), (heare/toyle)*   *(g)*

---

14. What heare shall <u>misse</u>, our <u>toyle</u> shall <u>strive</u> to <u>mend</u>.
*(repeated m "patient ears attend" is amplified, or
explained by "our toyle shall strive to mend.")*   *(g)*

Oral Exercise:
Communicate for Meaning

Work through the Chorus speech aloud, concentrating on the elements we have explored.

First, and most important: be specific and clear about the meaning of ideas.

Second, and of near-equal importance: learn to use the language's most important words, the verbs, as the key words, and the nouns as almost equally important words. Syncopate for meaning.

Recognize the balances and contrasts, and give them full emphasis; they help communicate meaning.

Acknowledge the poetic devices, such as rhyme and repeated sounds, but emphasize for meaning. Devices such as rhyme, deserve recognition, but meaning for the listener will be achieved through verbs, nouns, and balances/contrasts.

Don't concern yourself yet with "acting" or believability. Focus on the need for stressing the words and phrases that carry the freight of meaning. Our system in this workbook exists to enhance the communication of oral meaning. It's not about demonstrating our command of poetic devices.

Make Informed Choices

We recognize that all this work (the researching of word meanings, the mark-up system, the need to identify verbs and nouns and syncopate them, the process of "bringing it all together,") can be intimidating. And, it can seem technical.

In a sense it is technical. But how else will you address the text? By guessing which words are important? By reading them aloud the way you would a non-verse text? No, obviously that won't work. There are some technical/mechanical steps you must go through in order to address the text confidently, sharing the meaning with clarity.

We recognize that you won't have time to do all this work for every speech, every line, in preparation for playing Romeo or Juliet; it's too time-consuming. But: if you do the work in this book, several times, concentrating on building habits, you will be ready to make *informed choices* rather than *inspired guesses.*

We assure you that this mark-up system is a proven tool that has helped actors and other speakers develop a system of their own for studying the script, with the goal of concentrating on clarity of communication aloud.

Before We Bring It All Together

We are almost ready to apply everything we've learned to a scene. Before we bring it all together, however, there are several aspects of Shakespeare's verse which we must address. Let's turn our attention to one of *Romeo and Juliet*'s best-known scenes: the first meeting of Romeo and Juliet, at the Capulet house, where Juliet's family is hosting friends, relatives, and Romeo's crowd—who have attended uninvited.

The following text is adapted from the "quarto" version of the play. In its original printing, the play had no act or scene divisions, but this moment is usually labeled Act I, scene 5. Again, the original text has no stage direction, but the tradition of the scene is that the guests are dancing, and Romeo approaches Juliet, perhaps taking her hand in his:

Romeo: [Taking Juliet's hand]

1. If I prophane with my unworthiest hand,   A

2. This holy shrine, the gentle sin is this,   B

3. My lips two blushing Pilgrims ready stand,   A

4. To smooth that rough touch, with a tender kisse.   B

Juliet:

5. Good Pilgrime, you do wrong your hand too much. C

6. Which mannerly devotion shewes in this,   D

7. For Saints have hands, that Pilgrims hands do tuch, C

8. And palme to palme, is holy Palmers kisse.   D

Romeo:

9. Have not Saints lips, and holy Palmers too?   E

Juliet:

10. I Pilgrim, lips that they must use in prayer.   F

Romeo:

11. O then deare Saint, let lips do what hands do,   E

12. They pray (grant thou) least faith turne to dispaire. F

Juliet:

13. Saints do not move, though grant for prayers sake. G

Romeo:

14. Then move not while my prayers effect I take: G

[kiss]

15. Thus from my lips, by thine my sin is purg'd.   H

Juliet:

16. Then have my lips the sin that they have tooke.   I

Romeo:

17. Sin from my lips? O trespasse sweetly urg'd: H

18. Give me my sin againe.

[kiss]

Juliet:

You kisse by th'booke.   I

Note that these two young people have followed, in their first meeting (a love at first-sight), the rhyme scheme of a sonnet in lines 1 through 14, and after their first kiss, they begin the pattern of what could be a new sonnet. They are inspired!

Coining and Borrowing

To "coin a phrase" is to invent a phrase that hasn't been used before. To "borrow a phrase" is to reach into a bank of quotable phrases, whether personal, literary or cultural. The act of reaching beyond the scope of ordinary conversation and either "coining" or "borrowing" phrases heightens the level of personal expression. Romeo, in inventing the phrase, "my lips, two blushing Pilgrims," has coined a phrase for Juliet, mostly to impress her. As you read the role of Romeo, let him invent the phrase with some pride, some showing off about the invention. That will enable Juliet to be impressed, and to recognize that this is a smart, quick young man who may be an intellectual match for her. This is a sign of their intelligence; after all, it takes intelligence to invent a sonnet when you're meeting the person you're beginning to fall in love with. Characters written in verse often have a much greater verbal capacity than the present-day speaker of ordinary intelligence. But, it is possible, through practice, to speak Shakespeare's verse with all the character's cleverness and quick thinking. The key is *practice*.

The imagery about pilgrims, saints, prayer, hands kissing/versus lips kissing, is invented in the moment by two exceptionally quick young people. The play is filled with this ability of characters, especially the young people, to be verbally inventive, in the moment, and in the search of emotional victories in their relationships.

Keeping meaning in mind, and rising to the challenge of characters' quick intelligence, read the scene aloud.

Contracted Sounds

In this scene there are certain words, which if pronounced in the usual, uncontracted manner, would work against the flow of the iambic pentameter.

Obviously, "unworthiest" in line one demands a decision; it can be pronounced un<u>WORTHiEST</u> (four syllables), or it can be shortened into three syllables: un<u>WORTH</u>'yist. Either choice can work, but our choice is the latter: shorten it to three syllables. Why? If it's given three syllables, the line has ten syllables; in other words, it's a "regular" line.

In the two examples below, the line is broken down into five feet using slash marks (/), and the feet are numbered one through five.

Usual Pronunciation

un WORTH i est:

The fifth foot is a beat too long to be an iamb. It's actually another type of foot known as a "anapest," but the technical names for such variances are not very important here. Say the line using the three pulses in the final foot:

Romeo:

1	2	3	4	5

If I / prophane / with my / unworth /i-est hand

Contracted Pronunciation

un WORTH yist:

The fifth foot is an iamb in this example. The word unworthiest has been contracted to unworth- yist, making this a "regular," ten-syllable line. Say this line and practice using the contracted form of the word:

Romeo:

1	2		3	4	5

If I / prophane / with my / unworth-/yist hand

Usual Pronunciation

BY the BOOK:

Romeo:

1	2	3

give me / my sinne / againe /

Juliet:

	4	5

/you kisse / by the book/

Contracted Pronunciation

By th'BOOK

Romeo:

1	2	3

give me / my sinne / againe /

Juliet:

	4	5

/you kisse / by th'book/

In Shakespeare's time, license was taken with elements like these contractions. It was an accepted part of creating the ten-syllable iambic pentameter line. You will note that line eighteen is shared between Romeo and Juliet. Romeo's "Give me my sin againe" takes six beats, or three iambs; Juliet responds with "You kisse by th'booke," a phrase of four beats or two iambs if you contract "by th'booke" into two beats, one iamb. Shakespeare does this contraction of two syllables into one occasionally in order to maintain the iambic pentameter. Did the audience hear it? We don't know! Will they hear it today? Perhaps.

Adding a Syllable, Part One: Completing a Line of Verse

The word "prayer" is used in two different ways in this scene. In Romeo's line it is pronounced as one syllable. In Juliet's line, it is necessary to pronounce it as two syllables in order to make a complete, ten-syllable line of verse.

Usual pronunciation of the word "prayer"

Romeo:

1	2	3	4	5

Then move/ not while / my prayer's /effect /I take

Expanded pronunciation (two syllables)

Juliet:

1	2	3	4	5

Saints do/ not move/ though grant/for pray/er's sake

Adding a Syllable, Part Two: The "Feminine" Ending

In the passage below, Romeo (a Montague) has just discovered that his family and friends have entered into a brawl with the Capulets. Notice that the word "created" adds an extra beat to the usual iambic pentameter rhythm. This is known as a "weak" or "feminine" ending. A "feminine" ending occurs when the verse follows the usual pattern through the first four feet, but in the fifth foot, there is a final weak syllable added to the iamb: taDA taDA taDA taDA taDA ta. Labelling a weak syllable as "feminine" seems inappropriate today, but this is the traditional term handed down to us. You may prefer to call it a "weak" ending.

Romeo:

... Heere's much to do with hate, but more with love:

Why then, O brawling love O loving hate,

O any thing, of nothing first created:

As in the example above, the word "it," at the end of Juliet's second line is a weak, or "feminine" ending.

Romeo:

O wilt thou leave me so unsatisfied?

Juliet:

What satisfaction can'st thou have tonight?

Romeo:

Th'exchange of thy loves faithful vow for mine.

Juliet:

I gave thee mine before thou did'st request it:

Important note: Because the word "O" appears so often in the speech above, it seems an opportune place to point out that "O" in Shakespeare is always given full value; it should be pronounced fully as a word, rather than "swallowing" the sound.

Oral Exercise: "Feminine" Endings

Read the two excerpts above, conscious of the weak or "feminine" endings.

Adding a Syllable, Part Three:
The "ed" Suffix

In Shakespeare's verse, the suffix "ed," as in the word "stained," is sometimes pronounced with an extra syllable. In the example below, the Prince of Verona scolds the Capulet and Montague households for engaging in a street brawl. Notice that for the word "stained" to fit into the rhythm of iambic pentameter, a syllable must be added; it must be pronounced "stain-ed."

Prince:

Rebellious subjects, enemies to peace,

Prophaners of this Neighbor-stained steele,

Later in the speech, the word "mistempered" does not require an added "ed" syllable. It fits the meter if it is pronounced in the usual way. Notice too, that the Folio text indicates this by spelling the word with an apostrophe: "mistemper'd."

Throw your mistemper'd weapons to the ground,

As mentioned above, some editions of Shakespeare's plays, including the Folio, use an apostrophe to indicate the "short" pronunciation of the "ed" suffix, as in "mistemper'd." When the "elongated" ending is called for however, the "ed" suffix is written out, as in "stained." The Folio is not one hundred per cent consistent in providing apostrophes for the "short" pronunciation, but you will be able to determine what to do with "ed" suffixes by feeling the pulse of iambic pentameter and making sure that the verse line consists of five iambic "feet."

Oral Exercise:
Contractions and Elongations

In this example from the famous "balcony scene," the meter demands that some words be elongated and some contracted. Speak the following lines aloud, paying attention to the rhythm of the verse. Pay attention to the contractions and "ed" suffixes noted in italics.

O speake againe bright angell, for thou art

As glorious to this night being ore my head
(contract glorious to two syllables: glor yus;), (contract being to one syllable: "beeng")

As is a winged messenger of heaven
(elongate winged to two syllables: wing-ed),
(the word "heaven" is either a one-syllable contraction: "heav'n," or a "feminine" ending. Which is it? You decide.)

Unto the white upturned wondering eyes
(elongate upturned to three syllables: up-turn-ed)

Of mortalls that fall backe to gaze on him,

Unstressed "Not"

The word "not" is usually unstressed in Shakespeare. It is tempting to stress "not," but the fact is, the merest utterance of this word will negate with great power: have not <u>gone</u>, will not <u>go</u>, shall not <u>go</u>, is not <u>going</u>, can not <u>go</u>.

Broken/Shared Lines Which Indicate a Pause or a Stage Direction

Below is an example of a "shared line." The line of verse is begun by one speaker and completed by the next speaker. In Shakespeare's plays, sometimes the shared line is clearly a signal for a quick, cue pick-up. Other times, it's a cue to pause. Here it seems to be a cue to pause for a second kiss. Notice how the two lines combine to create one complete line of verse, ten beats of iambic pentameter.

Romeo:

1 2 3
Give me / my sin / againe. / [*they kiss*]

Juliet:

4 5
You kisse / by th'booke.

Broken/Shared Lines Which Indicate a Quick Cue Pick-Up

Here is another example of a "shared line." In this example the line is literally shared, rhythmically. It does not indicate a pause in which an action will take place, such as the kiss, above. It should flow seamlessly from the rhythm of the first speaker's line-beginning, into the second speaker's line-ending.

Romeo:

1   2   3

I dreamt/ a dream/ tonight.

Mercutio:

                4   5

                Well so / did I.

Romeo:

1   2

Well what / was yours?

Mercutio:

                3   4   5

                That dream/-ers oft/-en lie.

Bracketed Stage Directions

Perhaps you noticed that we introduced stage directions for the kisses. There were no stage directions for the kisses in the original folio and quarto text. Shakespeare's early printings seldom include stage directions for such actions. When you see an item bracketed [ ] in a Shakespeare text, it indicates that the bracketed item did not appear in the original text; it is rather an insertion into the text by an editor. Here are a few examples of stage directions which were added to the text by later editors:

In line one of Romeo and Juliet's sonnet, there is little doubt that Romeo takes Juliet by the hand, however, Shakespeare did not indicate this in the original text. It was a stage direction added by a later editor:

1. If I prophane with my unworthiest hand, [Romeo takes Juliet's hand]

It is certain that Romeo kisses Juliet at the end of line 14, however, Shakespeare did not write this stage direction in the original texts, it was added by a later editor:

14. Then move not while my prayers effect I take: [kiss]

Again, it is clear that Romeo and Juliet kiss at this point, but Shakespeare's original texts do not give this stage direction. It is added by a later editor:

18. Give me my sin againe. [kiss]

Juliet: You kisse by th'booke.

Implied Stage Directions

Part of learning to act in Shakespeare, including *speaking* Shakespeare, is the task of finding implied stage directions in the text. Here are places in the text where there are implied stage directions.

Romeo:

1. If I prophane with my unworthiest hand,   A
(There's no stage direction that he "approaches" her, but clearly he's speaking to her; after all, she answers in line five. He's speaking about her hand. Perhaps he's offering to kiss her hand. Clearly he's talking about smoothing his "touch" with a "tender kisse.")

2. This holy shrine, the gentle sin is this,   B
(What's the "holy shrine"? Her hand.)

3. My lips two blushing Pilgrims ready stand,   A
(In the play's culture, to be talented with words is to be sexy, attractive. So, to make himself attractive to her he "coins" a metaphor.)

4. To smooth that rough touch, with a tender kisse.   B
(He's being self-deprecating by calling his lips "rough." Isn't this a stage direction for his lips to approach her hand?)

Juliet:

5. Good Pilgrime, you do wrong your hand too much. C

(In line eight below, she suggests that touching palms is the way "holy Palmers kiss." So, if she's suggesting that Palmers (religious Pilgrims) kiss palm to palm, perhaps she's *showing* him her palm, face-out to his, a stage direction. But before she can do that, she either has to have allowed him to kiss her hand, or she must withdraw it before he kisses it. It's up to the actors, but there seems to be a *stage direction here*: sometime between line one and line eight he's offered to kiss her hand, she's withdrawn it, and she's offered a palm to palm.

There's another stage direction: she's picked up on his use of "hand" and "pilgrim." It's up to the actress to "return" those words with some sense that she heard his meaning, and is giving the words back with additional meaning.)

6. Which mannerly devotion shewes in this,   D

7. For Saints have hands, that Pilgrims hands do tuch, C
(She introduces the image that we're going to play with later in the scene: the statues of "saints" placed along religious Pilgrims' paths for the kissing or touching of their hands.)

8. And palme to palme, is holy Palmers kisse.   D
(Shakespeare loved puns. The actress has to recognize that she's using "palme" and "Palmers" with double meaning that she hopes he's smart enough to hear and appreciate.)

Romeo:

9. Have not Saints lips, and holy Palmers too?   E
(He's sharp enough to pick up her pun. But, also the implied or hidden stage direction is that he hears it, and comes back

quickly with the notion that these statues have lips to kiss with. Maybe it's even a stage direction to move in for a kiss.)

Juliet:

10. I Pilgrim, lips that they must use in prayer.   F
(The clear stage direction here is that she must read him quickly, and have an answer.)

Romeo:

11. O then deare Saint, let lips do what hands do,   E
(The stage direction: he's quick too. He picks up on the saint-hand image and...)

12. They pray (grant thou) least faith turne to dispaire. F
(...he comes up with the image of prayer as kiss. See, the direction clearly is that these people think quickly on their feet and love answering each other in a witty fashion.)

Juliet:

13. Saints do not move, though grant for prayers sake. G
(What's the stage direction? She's been charmed by his prayer-kiss image. Immediately she says, "Ok, you're quick, and you're right. I'll follow-up the image of the saint. They—statues of saints—stand still and let themselves be

kissed." So, she's indicating that she won't move in for a kiss, but like a statue she'll *let herself* be kissed.)

Romeo:

14. Then move not while my prayers effect I take: G
[kiss]
(He got the hint, and the stage direction in the line is that he's going to move in for the kiss.)

15. Thus from my lips, by thine my sin is purg'd.   H
(After the wonder and joy of the kiss, he's quick enough to return to the imagery they've been playing with: sinners, saints, and the kiss as an act of cleansing.)

Juliet:

16. Then have my lips the sin that they have tooke.   I
(She, of course, continues the image: "now I have the sin!")

Romeo:

17. Sin from my lips? O trespasse sweetly urg'd: H
(How lucky can I be, it's an invitation to another kiss.)

18. Give me my sin againe.
(Clearly the line says he wants to kiss her again, and he's gotten what he'll take as an invitation. So he kisses her.)

Juliet:

You kisse by th'booke.   I
(The line can be interpreted variously, but one guess is
that it's a stage direction that she lets him know she enjoyed
the kiss.)

Applying the Three Steps to a Scene

Step One: Test Your Understanding

Word Meanings

"prophane"

Prophane is used here as a verb. When we search for it in the *OED*, we find this is a variant spelling of our contemporary verb, "to profane," and that its first meaning is "to treat what is sacred with irreverence." There are multiple nuances of meaning for the verb, but the key concept here is that Romeo, in taking her hand, acknowledges he may be profaning a "holy shrine." He is treating her hand, a "holy shrine," in an irreverent way.

"gentle"

This is a terrific example of a word usage over which scholars have failed for centuries to agree. The *OED* offers several examples of the word, "gentle," being used in connection with gentlemanly behavior. The *OED* even cites examples from Shakespeare; but they leave this meaning unaddressed. We suppose the meaning has some relationship to gentlemanly or mannerly behavior; or, that a "gentle" sin is a sin of a minor sort.

"Pilgrim"

Romeo and Juliet bat the term "pilgrim" back and forth. It becomes a controlling image in their dialogue.

In the Middle Ages, the 11th, 12th, and 13th centuries especially, Christians made pilgrimages, trips, to the Holy Land as part of a series of "Crusades." The *OED* defines a pilgrim as a traveler, "one who journeys (usually over a long distance) to [a] sacred place, as an act of devotion."

In Roman Catholic worship, these pilgrims often stopped along the way to worship at "holy shrines" that contained statues of saints. Part of venerating the saint sometimes included kissing the saint.

"Palm"/"Palmer"

The palm leaf was the symbol of the "Palmer," an honorific name for a person who had made the trip to the Holy Land during the Crusades. Persons who had made the trip were entitled to wear a sign of a palm leaf, signifying their religious accomplishment and devotion.

Paraphrase

Using these clues, begin your paraphrase of the scene. Of course, there are other words you may need to look up (ideally in the *OED*). Write out your paraphrase, line-by-line, below. (We've given you space between the lines.) Then compare your paraphrase with ours on the next pages.

Exercise: Your Paraphrase

Write your own paraphrase in the space provided.

Romeo:
[Romeo takes Juliet's hand]

1. If I prophane with my unworthiest hand,   A

2. This holy shrine, the gentle sin is this,   B

3. My lips two blushing Pilgrims ready stand,   A

4. To smooth that rough touch, with a tender kisse.   B

Juliet:

5. Good Pilgrime, you do wrong your hand too much.   C

6. Which mannerly devotion shewes in this,   D

7. For Saints have hands, that Pilgrims hands do tuch,   C

8. And palme to palme, is holy Palmers kisse.   D

Romeo:

9. Have not Saints lips, and holy Palmers too?   E

Juliet:

10. I Pilgrim, lips that they must use in prayer.   F

Romeo:

11. O then deare Saint, let lips do what hands do,   E

12. They pray (grant thou) least faith turne to dispaire. F

Juliet:

13. Saints do not move, though grant for prayers sake. G

Romeo:

14. Then move not while my prayers effect I take: G
          [They kiss]

15. Thus from my lips, by thine my sin is purg'd.   H

Juliet:

16. Then have my lips the sin that they have tooke.   I

Romeo:

17. Sin from my lips? O trespasse sweetly urg'd: H

18. Give me my sin againe.
                    [They kiss again]

Juliet:

                        You kisse by th'booke.   I

Our Paraphrase

Compare your paraphrase and ours. Substitute your phrasing if it's more useful than ours; the critical issue is to have worked through it, idea by idea, making certain you understand. We find that the literal act of paraphrasing is useful for most people when they begin this process.

Romeo:
[Romeo takes Juliet's hand]

1. If I prophane with my unworthiest hand,   A
If I desecrate with my inadequate hand,

2. This holy shrine, the gentle sin is this,   B
This place of worship, the honorable offense is this,

3. My lips two blushing Pilgrims ready stand,   A
My lips, worshipful travelers that are pink with blood, are ready

4. To smooth that rough touch, with a tender kisse.   B
To correct the offense of touching the hand, with a kiss on the hand.

Juliet:

5. Good Pilgrime, you do wrong your hand too much.   C
Worthy traveler, you give inadequate honor to your hand.

6. Which mannerly devotion shewes in this,   D
The fashionably courteous gesture is illustrated by this,

7. For Saints have hands, that Pilgrims hands do tuch, C
Because religious statues have hands that worshipful travelers' hands touch,

8. And palme to palme, is holy Palmers kisse.   D
And you know that Pilgrim/Palmers kiss by touching hands palm to palm.

Romeo:

9. Have not Saints lips, and holy Palmers too?   E
But surely sainted ones have lips, and travelers do too?

Juliet:

10. I Pilgrim, lips that they must use in prayer.   F
Yes, traveler, but they reserve their lips for worship.

Romeo:

11. O then deare Saint, let lips do what hands do,   E
But worshiped object, let lips act in the manner hands act:

12. They pray (grant thou) least faith turne to dispaire. F
They speak prayers (give your lips away) so that belief is not disappointed.

Juliet:

13. Saints do not move, though grant for prayers sake. G
Statues of saints do not move, but they do grant the things asked for in prayer.

Note: Prayer in Shakespeare is often pronounced as two syllables. In line thirteen it's two; in fourteen, it's one.

Romeo:

14. Then move not while my prayers effect I take: G
                    [They kiss]
So, you hold still while I'll take what I've prayed for:

15. Thus from my lips, by thine my sin is purg'd.   H
See, my sin is taken away by having kissed your lips.

Juliet:

16. Then have my lips the sin that they have tooke.   I
But by taking it away from yours, mine got the sin.

Romeo:

17. Sin from my lips? O trespasse sweetly urg'd:　　H
You got it from my lips? Then I get the invitation.

18. Give me my sin againe. [They kiss again]
I'll take my sin back.

Juliet:

　　　　　　　　　　You kisse by th'booke.　　I
*You kiss as though you've read the book on gentlemanly
behavior!*
　　book = good book? (Implies he kisses well!)

Oral Exercise: Be Intelligent

After paraphrasing, read the scene aloud with a partner, keeping in mind the importance of communicating meaning, especially paying attention to the word play between Romeo and Juliet.

Rise to the characters' level of *intelligence*. Let them be interested enough in words and the power of words so that they can "coin" and "borrow" phrases.

Step Two: Stress for Meaning

1) <u>identify</u> the <u>verbs</u> (other than forms of "to be") and <u>underline</u> them twice; <u>identify</u> the <u>nouns</u> and <u>underline</u> them once;

2) <u>identify</u> the <u>contrasts</u> and <u>balances</u> (you may <u>want</u> to <u>circle</u> them, or <u>note</u> them in the <u>margin</u>);

3) however you do it, <u>concentrate</u> on <u>finding</u> your <u>way</u> to "<u>score</u>" the text for <u>speaking</u> it aloud with a clear <u>sense</u> of <u>communication</u>. Our <u>version</u> of the <u>mark-up</u> is on pages 114–117.

Step Three: Celebrate the Poetry

Find the repeated sounds. Notice them, but don't let the rhyme take over.

Exercise: Your Mark-Up

"The Sonnet" from Romeo and Juliet

Underlining of Verbs, Nouns

Repeated Sounds

Rhyme Scheme

Amplifying, Explaining, and Contrasting Words, and Other Clues

Romeo:

1. If I prophane with my unworthiest hand,   A

2. This holy shrine, the gentle sin is this,   B

3. My lips two blushing Pilgrims ready stand,   A

4. To smooth that rough touch with a tender kisse.   B

Juliet:

5. Good Pilgrime, you do wrong your hand too much. C

6. Which mannerly devotion shewes in this,   D

7. For Saints have hands, that Pilgrims hands do tuch,   C

8. And palme to palme, is holy Palmers kisse.   D

Romeo:

9. Have not Saints lips, and holy Palmers too?   E

Juliet:

10. I Pilgrim, lips that they must use in prayer.   F

Romeo:

11. O then, deare Saint, let lips do what hands do,   E

12. They pray (grant thou) least faith turne to dispaire. F

Juliet:

13. Saints do not move, though grant for prayers sake. G

Romeo:

14. Then move not while my prayers effect I take: G

15. Thus from my lips, by thine, my sin is purg'd.   H

Juliet:

16. Then have my lips the sin that they have tooke.   I

Romeo:

17. Sin from my lips? O tresspasse sweetly urg'd   H

18. Give me my sin againe.

Juliet:

           You kisse by th'booke   I

Our Mark-Up
"The Sonnet" from Romeo and Juliet
Underlining of Verbs, Nouns
Repeated Sounds
Rhyme Scheme
Amplifying, Explaining, and Contrasting Words, and Other Clues

Romeo:

1. If I <u>prophane</u> with my unworthiest <u>hand</u>,   A

2. This holy <u>shrine</u>, the gentle <u>sin</u> is this,   B
s s
treat 'holy shrine' as one noun

3. My <u>lips</u> two blushing <u>Pilgrims</u> ready <u>stand</u>,   A
s s s
Romeo "coins" the image of his lips as "two blushing pilgrims"

4. To <u>smooth</u> that rough <u>touch</u> with a tender <u>kisse</u>.   B
t t
contrast "rough touch" with "tender kisse"

Juliet:

5. Good <u>Pilgrime</u>, you do <u>wrong</u> your <u>hand</u> too much. C

6. Which mannerly <u>devotion</u> <u>shewes</u> in this,   D
sh sh

7. For <u>Saints</u> <u>have</u> <u>hands</u>, that <u>Pilgrims</u> <u>hands</u> do <u>tuch</u>, C

s s

z z z

"Saints hands" contrasts with "Pilgrim's hands"—in order to highlight this contrast, give the verb "have" less stress than usual.

8. And <u>palme</u> to <u>palme</u>, is holy <u>Palmers</u> <u>kisse</u>.   D

p p p

Romeo:

9. <u>Have</u> not <u>Saints</u> <u>lips</u>, and holy <u>Palmers</u> too?   E

s s s

Have stressed verb in unstressed position

Juliet:

10. I <u>Pilgrim</u>, <u>lips</u> that they must <u>use</u> in <u>prayer</u>.   F

Romeo:

11. O then, deare <u>Saint</u>, <u>let</u> <u>lips</u> <u>do</u> what <u>hands</u> <u>do</u>,   E

l l

s s

'O' is given full value as a word in Shakespeare.
Contrast: Lips do/hands do

12. They <u>pray</u> (<u>grant</u> thou) least <u>faith</u> <u>turne</u> to <u>dispaire</u>. F

faith/turn/dispaire

Juliet:

13. <u>Saints</u> do not <u>move</u>, though <u>grant</u> for <u>prayers</u> <u>sake</u>. G
s s s
stressed noun, (saints) in unstressed position
Contrast: image of Saints move / Saints grant

Romeo:

14. Then <u>move</u> not while my <u>prayers</u> <u>effect</u> I <u>take</u>:   G

15. Thus from my <u>lips</u>, by thine, my <u>sin</u> is <u>purg'd</u>.   H
s s s
Contrast: from my lips / by thine
Repeated sound: my by my

Juliet:

16. Then <u>have</u> my <u>lips</u> the <u>sin</u> that they have <u>tooke</u>.   I
s s
Balance: have lips / sin tooke

Romeo:

17. <u>Sin</u> from my <u>lips</u>? O <u>trespasse</u> sweetly <u>urg'd</u>:   H
s s s s s
Sin = noun in unstressed position

18. <u>Give</u> me my <u>sin</u> againe.
give = verb in unstressed position
Broken line = pause for kiss

Juliet:

You <u>kisse</u> by th'<u>booke</u>.   I

s

Note: No stage direction for first or second kiss

Oral Exercise:
Bringing It All Together

After comparing your mark-up with ours, your next step is to read the dialogue aloud, perhaps reading one part opposite a partner who has done the mark-up, perhaps reading both parts. Remember, your concentration is on speaking the text with great clarity of communication.

Part of the communication process, though, is keeping the characters' thought processes in mind, letting the characters "hear" what is said, and responding. If you are working with a partner, concentrate on "hearing" the use of words, and responding to the words used. Much of this scene involves "word play." Romeo speaks in his first speech about "hand" and "pilgrim." Juliet picks up on those images, and serves them back to him, playfully.

These two young people are bright, sexy, and interested in words.

Acting the Text:
Shakespeare's Demands

Up to now, we have concentrated on the technical aspects of Shakespeare's text: finding word meanings, exploring stresses, interpreting punctuation. In other words, we've worked on the process of finding the text's meaning and communicating it.

Now we want to explore a few key principles involved in understanding the Shakespearean text and acting it.

The Technical and the Creative

We will explore how to merge the technical processes with the creative process. That is, how does the actor blend the "technical problems" posed by archaic language and verse with the "creative problem" of playing a character who is involved in a relationship with other characters? Today's actors are often put off, intimidated, by the problem of integrating the technical and the creative. We want to help you master the "technical" and then merge the technical with the personal. We want the kind of Shakespearean acting that you want: acting in which we believe in the personal involvement of characters in the given circumstances of the play.

Stimulus-Response-Stimulus (S/R/S)

Our beginning concept is simple: In our everyday lives, we are constantly involved in "units" of experience that consist of a "stimulus" followed by a "response" to the stimulus. Each stimulus provokes a response; out of that response comes a new stimulus and its response and a new stimulus. Let's call it an S/R/S system.

1. Sometimes the process happens between people: what I say stimulates a reaction from you; your reaction, in turn, stimulates a response from me. (It's a simple concept; it sounds easy. But it's also too easy to make Shakespeare's characters into people who merely *talk*. They must *talk* and *think*. They *experience* and *respond*.

2. Sometimes the S/R/S happens in my mind: a stimulus causes me to respond; in turn there's a new stimulus, and a new response.

Think about how you think. Isn't it all a series of S/R/S?

I see ...

I respond to what I see ...

That reminds me of something about what I see ...
The reminder motivates me to a new thought ...
It's associational. It's the way my mind works. It's the way yours works and the way characters' minds work in the plays.

S/R/S and the "Balcony Scene"

Our next step is to illustrate this S/R/S process in the "Balcony Scene," (Act II, Scene ii). We're going to follow Romeo's S/R/S process through the beginning of the scene.

The given circumstances: Romeo has hidden in the shadows. He's listening to Mercutio and Benvolio taunt him with lewd sexual remarks, ridiculing Romeo's being in love with being in love. Eventually they give up and leave. Romeo enters from the darkness where he's been hiding:

Stimulus: Romeo believes they've left, so he re-joins the audience. He sees that we're still there, and his friends aren't.

Response: Romeo speaks to us.

Romeo: He jeasts at Scarres that never felt a wound,

Romeo is speaking to us, the audience, about his friends who have been making fun of him; he coins an image: it's easy to make fun of battle scars if you've never been wounded in battle.

Stimulus: He turns from us, and looks at a nearby balcony where there is a light coming from inside the house.

Response: Seeing the light motivates him to silence us. He asks a rhetorical question:

Romeo: But soft, what light through yonder window breaks?

The instruction was for us to be quiet. The question is rhetorical: he doesn't want an answer.

Stimulus: In the act of asking the question, he coins his own metaphorical answer:

Response: The balcony stands to the east where the sun rises each morning; and, supposing it could be Juliet's window, he coins a metaphor:

Romeo: It is the East, and Juliet is the Sunne,

Stimulus: He is stimulated by his own words and the mental connection between the light and Juliet. He follows the premise of his own metaphor.

Response: He addresses the light. Juliet is not there, so he's asking her, the sun, to rise:

Romeo: Arise faire Sun and kill the envious Moone,

Stimulus: Romeo's reference bank is different from ours. Like many of Shakespeare's characters, he knows Greek and Roman mythology. He knows that in the Roman deity system, Diana was the moon goddess, a determined virgin. In Shakespeare's time there was a notion of a "sickness" associated with pubescent girls: moonsickness. The common wisdom was that they turned green because of the absence of a husband. Romeo's mind has created the metaphor of Juliet representing the sun, then the moon as the sun's opponent. He imagines Juliet as a "maid" of the moon, assuming her to be a virgin. The clothing that the vestal virgins wear is "sick and green" (the color of greensickness), and only a foolish person would align herself with such a goddess.

Response: Romeo continues his metaphor:

Romeo: Who is already sicke and pale with griefe,
That thou her Maid art far more faire than she:
Be not her Maid since she is envious,
Her Vestal livery is but sicke and greene,
And none but fooles do weare it,

Stimulus: He thinks of her being a Vestal virgin, and wants her to give that up.

Response: He urges her not to be maid to Diana the moon goddess of virginity.

Romeo: ... cast it off:

Throughout this passage, Romeo has been addressing an imaginary Juliet on the balcony, all the while aware of our presence because he addressed us earlier. There is no stage direction in the Folio version of Romeo and Juliet, but we can presume she enters after "cast it off," because in his next line he says:

Romeo: It is my Lady, O it is my Love,

Stimulus: He sees her.

Response: He speaks to us; we are his compatriots, almost a rooting section he can count on to support him. He tells us it's Juliet, even though he knows we know. And he knows we're aware she's his love; the new information he feeds us is that he wishes she knew of his love.

Romeo: O that she knew she were,

Stimulus: Next, he looks back to her, and sees her moving her lips.

Response: That stimulates him to say:

Romeo: She speakes, yet she sayes nothing, what of that?

He's telling us to observe that she's moving her lips but not vocalizing, and he asks us what to make of it. (Juliet, we must assume, is thinking about Romeo, whom she's met and fallen in love with at the ball, and she's murmuring something about him that he and we can't hear.)

Stimulus: He turns back to look at her, observes that she's still not speaking aloud.

Response: In the urgency of his need to speak with her, he turns back to tell us her eye is speaking, so he'll answer it.

Romeo: Her eye discourses, I will answere it:

Stimulus: Immediately he recognizes that he's being overly forward, and is only presuming she's speaking to him.

Response: He acknowledges to us his forwardness:

Romeo: I am too bold 'tis not to me she speakes:

Stimulus: In the depth of that temporary disappoint-ment, he has a new idea: He observes two very bright stars in the sky and "coins" a metaphor for Juliet's eyes.

Response: He proposes to us that we imagine there are two stars out there in the night sky that need to run an errand, and they ask her eyes to take their place in the sky and do their twinkling until they get back.

Romeo: Two of the fairest starres in all the Heaven,
Having some business do entreat her eyes,
To twinckle in their Spheres till they returne.

Stimulus: In sharing with us the idea of her eyes being out there twinkling, shining, he comes up with a new idea based on the previous one: what if her eyes were out there in the sky, shining; and what if the stars were located "in her head," in her eye sockets?

Response: He already has an answer; he responds to his own thought as stimulus: her eyes would be so bright, so powerful, shining from out there in the night sky, that the reflection off her cheek would overwhelm the power of two mere stars. And, while he's telling us he gets carried away with enthusiasm, with passion. He proposes to us that her eyes would create light so bright that the birds would wake up and sing, thinking it's morning.

Romeo: What if her eyes were there, they in her head[?]
The brightness of her cheeke would shame those starres,

As day-light doth a Lampe, her eye in heaven,
Would through the ayrie Region streame so bright,
That Birds would sing, and thinke it were not night:

Stimulus: And now his mind shifts. Why? Because Juliet has leaned over the balcony ledge, and put her chin in her hand. There is no stage direction in the Folio; we must find the stage direction as we do so often in Shakespeare: through the text, through what the characters say. He's so enthralled with love that he thinks she does this simple act with greater beauty than any other woman could.

Response: He asks us to look at it, appreciate it. Then he follows up with a wish he shares aloud with us: that he could be a glove on the hand that touches the cheek. He says to us:

Romeo: See how she leanes her cheeke upon her hand.
O that I were a Glove upon that hand,
That I might touch that cheeke.

Stimulus: Meanwhile, Juliet is thinking of Romeo. She thinks how sad it is that he's a Montague, a family against which her family has a long-standing grudge.

Response: She uses a familiar exclamation to voice her turmoil.

Juliet: Ay me.

Where Have We Been?
What Have We Done?

The process we just took you through in the "balcony scene" is not in essence different from interpreting a contemporary play text. The difficulty lies in learning how to develop a thought process for the character that grows out of the text. Your work must be specific. The thoughts must be based in the text. It's difficult because it's hard work. If you fake it, we won't know what you're talking about. We'll merely become bored.

Is it "technical"? To some degree, yes. It's technical to the degree that the Shakespearean acting process requires work we aren't used to doing.

Some Additional Thoughts on Acting Shakespeare

1. Use language to get what you want. A major difference between acting many contemporary plays and Shakespeare's is that Shakespeare's characters are more empowered by language. Language was power in Elizabethan England. Shakespeare's characters use language as a tool to gain what they want: sex, power, money. Obviously that's different from some parts of our contemporary American culture in which many people "like, don't even try to use language as an obvious inter-personal tool."

2. Speak Shakespeare with your own voice, your own speech. Students with foreign or regional accents should dive right in with their accented English. Most actors in Shakespeare's time almost certainly didn't speak upper-class English. They spoke with regional accents. Your speech and voice are just fine, thanks.

3. Think fast, but don't speak fast. Shakespeare's poetry lends itself to the actor thinking rapidly and not "fumbling" or searching for words. Shakespeare's characters think and speak "on the word" not "between" the words. Extra pauses to gather your thoughts will, in fact, cause us to lose the character's thought process.

4. Allow your character to think in an organized fashion. Let her/him state the premise of the argument, and then build a series of logical thoughts. This isn't an affectation. It's the way Shakespeare's characters think.

5. If the character's thought process doesn't seem logical, ask yourself: Is there a dramatic reason? An emotional reason?

6. Relax and breathe fully, deeply.

7. Avoid unnecessary breaths; if the idea continues, try to do it in a breath that holds out through the idea. Take little "catch breaths" in order to keep the ideas flowing. Of course, it helps if you've expanded your breath capacity.

8. Connect your breathing to the character's thinking. "Breathe in" the text, the images, the action. Keep the solar plexus area free, relaxed.

9. Speak clearly. This is crucial to being understood on stage. Most students must work long and hard to achieve beginning, middle and final consonant sounds which are sharp and energetic. In speaking Shakespeare, the consonants "fling" the vowels forward. Audience members watch the face and even read the lips to help them "hear" what you're saying; so keep your face mobile, your sound forward and your consonants crisp so they can follow. After all, the play's being done for them.

Pronunciation

Today's American theatre faces a dilemma as to the best way to pronounce words in Shakespeare. Is it acceptable to use one's own accent? Is it better to sound "Shakespearean," or British? Incredibly, some American actors actually use a British accent when performing Shakespeare. Others use a kind of stage-speech which is not entirely British, but has some British characteristics. This dilemma is reinforced by the fact that most performances of Shakespeare's plays on video and audio recordings feature British performers. Americans see this British Shakespeare and think that's how they should speak. It is our conviction that ordinary American pronunciation is the most appropriate way for American actors to speak Shakespeare.

Even so, sometimes the pronunciation of a word may be altered in order to maximize communication. We recommend a general rule: If the meter dictates a pronunciation which is difficult for the audience to comprehend, sacrifice the meter for the accessible pronunciation.

Here are a few examples of specific words for which more than one pronunciation choice exists:

How should the word "lamentable" be pronounced? `la men ta ble, or, la `men ta ble? In Shakespeare's texts this word scans as `la men ta ble, however, this may be difficult for some modern ears to comprehend because there is a current trend to pronounce this word as la `men ta ble.

What about the word "detestable"? It is interesting that in *Romeo and Juliet* this word scans as `de tes ta ble, rather than the modern pronunciation de `tes ta ble. However it is preferable to pronounce this word as de `tes ta ble. It helps the audience to comprehend the meaning.

We have just the opposite problem with the word "presage." In *Romeo and Juliet* this word scans as pre `sage, but the current dictionary pronunciation is `pre sage. In this case, an audience is likely to guess the meaning of this word, which differs from the current "correct" pronunciation. Common sense tells us that "pre," (meaning before) and "sage," (meaning wise), when put together would mean to "predict," or have a premonition of some future event or circumstance.

Directors of *King Lear* often insist that the word "revenue" be pronounced re `ven ue. However, this sounds so different from the present-day pronunciation `re ve nue that it could easily be incomprehensible to the listener. An interesting parallel is that in a later speech in *King Lear*, the word retinue scans as re `ti nue, but we are unaware of a director favoring that pronunciation over the more commonly heard `re ti nue. Common sense will usually tell you when it is necessary to sacrifice the meter in order to pronounce words in an accessible way for the audience. In a sentence: make the choice that helps the audience attend to the play rather than your pronunciation. Make the less distracting choice.

Spelling

Earlier, we suggested that spelling in Shakespeare's England was a "creative act." For Shakespeare and his contemporaries, English was in the process of being standardized; there were no pronouncing dictionaries. There was not yet a strong concept of correct and incorrect spellings.

In the ensuing four hundred years, some words have changed their spellings. Here is a sampling of words that were spelled differently in Shakespeare's day; we've given the contemporary American spelling, followed by the Elizabethan one:

suit/sute; scarf/skarfe; waste/wast; chaste/chast; taste/tast; haste/hast; dew/deaw; master/maister; ancient/auncient; Montague/Mountague; matched/macht; touch/tuch; two/to; air/ayre; girl/gyrle; dirges/dyrges; again/agen; heart/hart; blood/bloud; enough/inough; Friar/Frier; than/then; iron/yron; curfew/curphew; scaring/skaring.

Inconsistencies of spelling reach such heights in Shakespeare that some words are spelled two different ways on the same page, even in the same character's speech:

Frier:
What, rowse thee man, thy Juliet is alive,
For whose deare sake thou wast but lately dead,
There art thou <u>happy</u>. Tybalt would kill thee,
But thou slew'st Tybalt. There art thou <u>happie</u>.

Juliet:
Tybalt is dead and Romeo banished:
That banished, that one word banished,
Hath slaine ten thousand Tibalts ...
etc ...

In the first scene of *Romeo and Juliet,* the word "we" receives two different spellings a mere line apart:

Sampson:
Gregory, A my word wee'l not carry coales.

Gregory:
No for then we should be Colliars.

The word Spite appears several times in *Romeo and Juliet,* spelled Spight:

Capulet:
My sword I say: Old Mountague is come,
And flourishes his blade in spight of me.

Paris:
Beguiled, divorced, wronged, spighted, slaine ...

The word Moved is spelled Mooved:

Prince:
...And heare the sentence of your mooved Prince.

In the First Folio, "than" is spelled as "then"; for example:

Romeo:
Alacke there lies more perill in thine eye,
THEN twenty of their swords, ...

In the first folio, the typesetters seem to have shortened spellings in order to save space. For example, the following sentence fits on one line, but would have taken up two lines if one more letter had been added. This may explain why the word "will" was spelled with one "l" rather than two:

Gregory:
I wil frown as I pass by, & let the[m] take it as they list.

The examples above, and many others like them, may provide the actor with clues for interpretation. For instance, the Prince, in an emotional state at the beginning of the play, refers to himself as "mooved," with two "O's" rather than "moved," with just one "O." Is this perhaps a way in which the playwright and/or typesetters are giving the actor a clue as to the intensity of his emotional state, and the way in which he ought to express it? To hang on to the vowel and say "mooved," provides an opportunity charge the word emotionally, or to make it more active.

Look through the folio and quarto editions of *Romeo and Juliet* for other clues of this sort.

Spelling and the Actor

What lesson or message should the contemporary actor take from this realization of such inconsistent spelling in the folio and the quartos? The best answer: be cautious. There are instances in which the spelling may be taken as a direction for the actor; but the spellings are so inconsistent that there are no certain stage directions to be found in them.

Selective Bibliography

Epstein, Norrie.
The Friendly Shakespeare: A Thoroughly Painless Guide to the Bard. New York: Penguin, 1994.

This is a breezy, informal book that answers many of the questions you were reluctant to ask in class.

Linklater, Kristin.
Freeing Shakespeare's Voice. New York: Theatre Communications Group, 1992.

Freeing the Natural Voice. New York: Drama Book Specialists, 1976.

We believe Linklater's books are the best place for the actor to read about the process of integrating breath, thought, and text.

Onions, C.T.
Glossary. London: Oxford University Press, 1986.

This is the best shortcut to finding the meanings of obscure words in Shakespeare. But, whenever possible, consult the *Oxford English Dictionary* (see below). It will help you understand usage in Shakespeare's time.

Papp, Joseph and Kirkland, Elizabeth.
Shakespeare Alive! New York: Bantam, 1988.
For the beginning student, this book provides an excellent orientation to Shakespeare and his times.

Schoenbaum, Samuel.
William Shakespeare: A Compact, Documentary Life. London: Oxford University Press, 1988.
This is the very best factual biography of Shakespeare. The "documentary" in the title refers to Schoenbaum's emphasis on the documented information of Shakespeare's life, rather than conjectures about his life.

Shakespeare, William.
The First Folio of Shakespeare, prepared by Charlton Hinman. New York: W. W, Norton, 1968.
You are likely to find this edition in your local library.

Shakespeare, William.
Mr. William Shakespeare's comedies, histories & tragedies: a facsimile of the first folio, 1623, Introduction by Doug Moston. New York: Routledge, 1998.
This is one of several first folio facsimilies in print.

Shakespeare, William.
Applause First Folio Editions, prepared and annotated by Neil Freeman.

New York: Applause Books, 1998, 1999, 2000.
This is a series of paperback acting editions of the plays. It uses the folio text printed in modern type-face.

Shakespeare, William.
The Riverside Shakespeare [complete works]. New York: Houghton Mifflin, 1997.
The Riverside's scholarship is excellent, and its introductory notes are clear and thorough.

Shakespeare, William.
Folger Shakespeare [individual plays]. Pocket Books, 1997.
The Folger Shakespeare series precedes each scene with a brief synopsis of the scene.

Shakespeare, William.
Arden Shakespeare [individual plays], edited by Eric Partridge. London: Oxford University Press, 1997.
The Arden Shakespeare series offers excellent scholarly notes.

Shakespeare, William.
Shakespeare's Bawdy. New York: Routledge, 1991.
If you want to know what the "sexy" or "dirty" parts mean, this is the book for you.

Simpson, J. A. and E. S. C. Weiner.
The Oxford English Dictionary. London: Oxford University Press, 1989.

Tillyard, E.M.W.

The Elizabethan World Picture. New York: Random House, 1959.

The book addresses what the Elizabethans believed about their world.

Books Available From Santa Monica Press

Blues for Bird
by Martin Gray
288 pages $16.95

The Book of Good Habits
Simple and Creative Ways to Enrich Your Life
by Dirk Mathison
224 pages $9.95

Café Nation
Coffee Folklore, Magick, and Divination
by Sandra Mizumoto Posey
224 pages $9.95

Collecting Sins
A Novel
by Steven Sobel
288 pages $13

FREE Stuff & Good Deals for Folks over 50
by Linda Bowman
240 pages $12.95

FREE Stuff & Good Deals for Your Pet
by Linda Bowman
240 pages $12.95

FREE Stuff & Good Deals on the Internet
by Linda Bowman
240 pages $12.95

Health Care Handbook
A Consumer's Guide to the American Health Care System
by Mark Cromer
256 pages $12.95

Helpful Household Hints
The Ultimate Guide to Housekeeping
by June King
224 pages $12.95

How to Find Your Family Roots and Write Your Family History
by William Latham and Cindy Higgins
288 pages $14.95

How to Speak Shakespeare
by Cal Pritner and Louis Colaianni
144 pages $16.95

How to Win Lotteries, Sweepstakes, and Contests in the 21st Century
by Steve "America's Sweepstakes King" Ledoux
224 pages $14.95

The Keystone Kid
Tales of Early Hollywood
by Coy Watson, Jr.
304 pages $24.95

Letter Writing Made Easy!
Featuring Sample Letters for Hundreds of Common Occasions
by Margaret McCarthy
224 pages $12.95

Letter Writing Made Easy! Volume 2
Featuring More Sample Letters for Hundreds of Common Occasions
by Margaret McCarthy
224 pages $12.95

Nancy Shavick's Tarot Universe
by Nancy Shavick
336 pages $15.95

Offbeat Food
Adventures in an Omnivorous World
by Alan Ridenour
240 pages $19.95

Offbeat Golf
A Swingin' Guide To a Worldwide Obsession
by Bob Loeffelbein
192 pages $17.95

Offbeat Marijuana
The Life and Times of the World's Grooviest Plant
by Saul Rubin
240 pages $19.95

Offbeat Museums
The Collections and Curators of America's Most Unusual Museums
by Saul Rubin
240 pages $19.95

Past Imperfect
How Tracing Your Family Medical History Can Save Your Life
by Carol Daus
240 pages $12.95

Quack!
Tales of Medical Fraud from the Museum of Questionable Medical Devices
by Bob McCoy
240 pages $19.95

The Seven Sacred Rites of Menarche
The Spiritual Journey of the Adolescent Girl
by Kristi Meisenbach Boylan
160 pages $11.95

The Seven Sacred Rites of Menopause
The Spiritual Journey to the Wise-Woman Years
by Kristi Meisenbach Boylan
144 pages $11.95

Silent Echoes
Discovering Early Hollywood Through the Films of Buster Keaton
by John Bengtson
240 pages $24.95

What's Buggin' You?
Michael Bohdan's Guide to Home Pest Control
by Michael Bohdan
256 pages $12.95

Order Form: 1-800-784-9553

	Quantity	Amount
Blues for Bird ($16.95)	_____	_____
The Book of Good Habits ($9.95)	_____	_____
Café Nation ($9.95)	_____	_____
Collecting Sins ($13)	_____	_____
FREE Stuff & Good Deals for Folks over 50 ($12.95)	_____	_____
FREE Stuff & Good Deals for Your Pet ($12.95)	_____	_____
FREE Stuff & Good Deals on the Internet ($12.95)	_____	_____
Health Care Handbook ($12.95)	_____	_____
Helpful Household Hints ($12.95)	_____	_____
How to Find Your Family Roots . . . ($14.95)	_____	_____
How to Speak Shakespeare ($16.95)	_____	_____
How to Win Lotteries, Sweepstakes, and Contests . . . ($14.95)	_____	_____
The Keystone Kid ($24.95)	_____	_____
Letter Writing Made Easy! ($12.95)	_____	_____
Letter Writing Made Easy! Volume 2 ($12.95)	_____	_____
Nancy Shavick's Tarot Universe ($15.95)	_____	_____
Offbeat Food ($19.95)	_____	_____
Offbeat Golf ($17.95)	_____	_____
Offbeat Marijuana ($19.95)	_____	_____
Offbeat Museums ($19.95)	_____	_____
Past Imperfect ($12.95)	_____	_____
Quack! ($19.95)	_____	_____
The Seven Sacred Rites of Menarche ($11.95)	_____	_____
The Seven Sacred Rites of Menopause ($11.95)	_____	_____
Silent Echoes ($24.95)	_____	_____
What's Buggin' You? ($12.95)	_____	_____

Shipping & Handling:		
1 book	$3.00	
Each additional book is	$ .50	

Subtotal _____

CA residents add 8% sales tax _____

Shipping and Handling (see left) _____

TOTAL _____

Name _____

Address _____

City _____ State _____ Zip _____

☐ Visa ☐ MasterCard   Card No.:_____

Exp. Date_____ Signature _____

☐ Enclosed is my check or money order payable to:

Santa Monica Press LLC
P.O. Box 1076
Santa Monica, CA 90406
www.santamonicapress.com

1-800-784-9553